Table of Contents

The First 109 Minutes: 9/11 and the U.S. Air Force

Introduction

Tuesday, September 11, 2001, dawned cool and clear, with sunny skies all along the eastern seaboard. For Air Force aviators like Lt. Col. Timothy "Duff" Duffy of the 102d Fighter Wing at Otis Air National Guard Base, Massachusetts, the day held the promise of perfect flying weather, at a time when the U.S. civil aviation system was enjoying a period of relative peace, despite concerns about a growing terrorist threat. More than ten years had passed since the last hijacking or bombing of a U.S. air carrier. That morning, however, the country came under a shocking, coordinated aerial assault by nineteen al Qaeda[1] hijackers at the direction of the network's leader and cofounder, Islamist extremist Osama bin Laden (1957/1958–2011).[2] The attack plan carried out by the suicide operatives had been years in the making. It was intended to cause mass, indiscriminate casualties and to destroy or damage the nation's financial, military, and political centers, four high-value U.S. targets selected by bin Laden, independent operator Khalid Sheikh Mohammed, and al Qaeda operations chief Mohammed Atef.[3] Analysts in the United States immediately recognized the historic nature of the strikes,[4] launched without warning against targets in New York City and Washington, D.C., and compared them to another deadly surprise aerial attack against the United States almost sixty years earlier.[5] The December 7, 1941, assault by Japanese forces on the U.S. naval base at Pearl Harbor had been the most devastating attack against U.S. territory by a foreign adversary until the morning of September 11, 2001.[6]

The four al Qaeda hijacker-pilots and their teams commandeered the four fuel-laden commercial jets in which they were passengers and intentionally crashed them into 1 and 2 World Trade Center, in New York City; the Pentagon, in Arlington, Virginia; and an empty field in Shanksville, Pennsylvania. This final hijacking, of United Airlines Flight 93, fell short of its intended target in Washington, D.C., because of heroic efforts by its passengers to take back control of the aircraft. The 9/11 attack, which began with the hijacking of American Airlines Flight 11 and was followed by the hijackings of United Airlines Flight 175, American Airlines Flight 77, and United Airlines Flight 93, would become, over the next two and a quarter hours, the deadliest, costliest terrorist strike in U.S. history. The 109-minute attack period itself began when American Airlines Flight 11 was attacked at or just after 8:14 a.m. Eastern Daylight Time (EDT). It ended when United Airlines Flight 93 crashed at 10:03 a.m. EDT, but the loss of life did not. By the time 1 World Trade Center, North Tower, collapsed at 10:28 a.m. EDT, almost three thousand people had been killed or were dying; the financial center of the United States had been reduced to burning, toxic rubble; the iconic symbol of the military strength of the country had been severely damaged; the tranquility of a field in Pennsylvania had been shattered; U.S. Air Force and Air National Guard fighter aircraft had set up combat air patrols over Washington, D.C., and New York City; and the administration of President George W. Bush and the Department of Defense (DOD) had begun shifting major resources of the federal government and military services to a new national priority, homeland defense.[7]

Even while the attacks were underway, it was clear that the country faced an unprecedented challenge. On the floor of the command center at the North American Aerospace Defense Command's (NORAD) Northeast Air Defense Sector (NEADS) in Rome, New York, SMSgt. Steve Bianchi, an assistant to mission crew commander Maj. Kevin J. Nasypany, reflected: "This is a new type of war."[8] And suddenly, as Vice President Richard Cheney noted a few days after the attacks, the country's national leadership had to consider a new mission for U.S. Air Force pilots: the possible shoot-down of commercial passenger aircraft filled with U.S. citizens.[9]

The terrorist attacks of September 11, 2001, had a profound impact on the nation's economy and governmental organization; on its budgets for national defense; and on the mission of its armed forces, particularly the U.S. Air Force. Even the date—9/11—quickly became iconic, and without the hijackings, the first three major U.S. military operations of the new century would not have been launched: Operation Noble Eagle, Operation Enduring Freedom, and Operation Iraqi Freedom. The U.S. Air Force has played an important role in all three. The 9/11 attacks precipitated the launch of Operation Noble Eagle and obliged the U.S. Air Force to deploy forces to protect the continental United States, Alaska, Canada, Hawaii, and Guam against additional air attacks.

The nature, timing, and effectiveness of the air defense response initiated by the Northeast Air Defense Sector on the morning of September 11 depended on many factors. Several were partly or entirely outside the control of the U.S. Air Force, such as the speed of the attacks and the tactics of the hijackers; the knowledge, experience, intuition, and initiative of Federal Aviation Administration (FAA) personnel; and the involvement and actions of those higher up the civilian chain of command. But the air defense response depended perhaps most on the effectiveness of the communications, coordination, and interaction *within and between* the FAA on the one hand and NORAD and NEADS on the other.[10]

NORAD Air Defense Structure on 9/11

On September 11, 2001, the North American Aerospace Defense Command, based at Peterson Air Force Base, Colorado, under the command of Gen. Ralph E. Eberhart, oversaw three air defense regions, which were responsible for protecting the airspace over Alaska, Canada, and the continental United States. The last of these, the Continental United States NORAD Region (CONR), under the command of the dual-hatted commander of First Air Force, Maj. Gen. Larry K. Arnold, oversaw the Northeast, the Western, and the Southeast Air Defense Sectors. The locations of the departures, flight paths, and crash sites of the four aircraft hijacked on September 11, 2001, were all in the Northeast Air Defense

Sector, commanded by Col. Robert K. Marr (*see* Diagram, NORAD Air Defense Structure on 9/11, p 53).

On September 11, 2001, the responsibility for defending continental U.S. airspace rested with only fourteen fighter aircraft at seven air defense alert sites across the country.[11] Based in Rome, New York, the Northeast Air Defense Sector had only two alert sites on which to call—Otis Air National Guard Base in Cape Cod, Massachusetts, and Langley Air Force Base in Hampton, Virginia. Each site had two designated alert fighters on duty twenty-four hours a day, seven days a week. Many other fighter aircraft were based across the country, but they were not NORAD assets, and it would take time to arm them and organize their crews.[12]

Earlier, far larger numbers of U.S. Air Force aircraft had provided air defense for the entire nation. The post-World War II chill in relations between the United States and the Soviet Union, the expansion of the Soviet long-range bomber fleet, and the detonation in 1949 of a Soviet atomic bomb contributed to the evolution of the continental air defense mission and its dedicated fighter force in the United States. Established in 1957, the joint U.S.-Canadian North American Air Defense Command, as it was then called, was responsible for intercepting any Soviet long-range bombers that might attack the Northern Hemisphere. The command's forces numbered about twelve hundred interceptors by 1960. The number of alert fighters and alert sites changed as the Soviet military threat evolved. In light of increased Soviet reliance on ballistic missiles over manned bombers beginning in the early 1960s, and because of budget constraints, the Department of Defense had by the mid-1970s reduced the number of NORAD interceptors to about three hundred. The number of alert sites and alert fighters continued to drop as the breakup of the Soviet Union and the dissolution of the Warsaw Pact in 1991 greatly diminished the threat of nuclear attack, which NORAD's core structure had been developed to counter. Thereafter, NORAD strategists began to consider shifting the mission from air defense against nuclear attack to defending the United States and Canada by maintaining peacetime air sovereignty. This meant "providing surveillance and control of the territorial airspace." To do so, NORAD air sovereignty fighters would carry out a number of missions. These included "intercepting and destroying uncontrollable air objects; tracking hijacked aircraft; assisting aircraft in distress; . . . and intercepting suspect aircraft, including counterdrug operations and peacetime military intercepts." In the early years after the fall of the Soviet Union, NORAD's leaders believed that the command's most pressing mission was intercepting drug smugglers. But, in fact, the largest percentage of alert sites' total activity involved assisting aircraft in distress and inspecting unidentified aircraft.[13]

In February 1993, Gen. Colin L. Powell, U.S. Army, the Chairman of the Joint Chiefs of Staff (CJCS), determined that because of the greatly lessened Soviet threat "the United States no longer needed a large, dedicated air defense force."[14] He therefore recommended that the number of dedicated Air National Guard units assigned to the continental air defense mission "be sharply reduced or eliminated" and that the mission be carried out "by dual tasking existing active and reserve general-purpose fighter and training squadrons in the Air Force, the Navy, and the Marine Corps."[15] In a report sent on May 3, 1994, to the chairmen of the U.S. Senate and U.S. House armed services committees and subcommittees on defense appropriations, the General Accounting Office—as the General Accountability Office was then called—supported Powell's recommendations, concluding, "A dedicated continental air defense force is no longer needed."[16]

Overview of the 9/11 Attacks and Summary of the Air Defense Response

The 9/11 terrorist attacks engendered the classic fog of war, in the air and on the ground. The government's longstanding antihijacking protocol, which set out the roles and responsibilities of the Federal Aviation Administration and the North American Aerospace Defense Command in the event of air piracy, was either bypassed or lost along its way to the Office of the Secretary of Defense. Amidst the chaos and violence of that morning, the U.S. Air Force played a prominent role in reacting to the attacks, as service personnel labored in the face of the nation's deadliest surprise attack since Pearl Harbor to defend the country against multiple commandeered aircraft and additional suspected hijackings.

Of critical importance to an effective air defense response was timely notification by FAA air traffic controllers to Northeast Air Defense Sector personnel of each hijacking. That issue and other aspects of the air defense response timeline were investigated by the National Commission on Terrorist Attacks Upon the United States—more commonly known as the 9/11 Commission—beginning in early 2003. The commission's investigations continued into 2004, and its final report was published in July of that year.[17]

The commission had access to extensive audio and written records, including various logs, tape recordings, and radar transmissions from NEADS, NORAD, CONR, and the FAA. These sources enabled the commission to determine, for the first time, an accurate timeline of the hijackings and the military response to them.[18] The reconstruction of the events of 9/11 had been faulty in the days immediately after the attacks and slow for some time thereafter. This was due, in part, to the complex, cascading nature of the attacks; their coordination; their speed; conflicting and incomplete accounts regarding possible follow-on hijackings; an overwhelming focus on preventing future attacks rather than immediately dissecting the reaction to the last one; and inadequate forensic capabilities across the government, particularly within key entities of the air defense response. The original faulty timelines, drafted by government agencies in the hours and days after the attacks, were the basis of widespread media coverage and congressional testimony. Their problematic nature became apparent even before the 9/11 Commission published its final report, and in March

2004, NORAD's commander, General Eberhart, wrote to the 9/11 Commission acknowledging that its timeline was accurate.[19]

In a finding of particular relevance to the U.S. Air Force and the conduct of future U.S. air defense operations, the commission concluded that the Federal Aviation Administration did not notify the Northeast Air Defense Sector of the hijackings expeditiously enough for Air Force fighters to intercept any of the doomed aircraft. This resulted from various circumstances, many having to do with the surprise nature of the attacks and the violent tactics of the hijackers. With respect to the four hijackings, the commission determined the following:

1. The FAA notified NEADS of the first hijacking—shortly thereafter determined to be American Airlines Flight 11—just under nine minutes before the plane slammed into the north tower of the World Trade Center. This was the longest notification NEADS air defenders received that day.[20]

2. The FAA notified NEADS of a "second possible hijack" almost simultaneously with the crash of United Airlines Flight 175 into the South Tower.[21]

3. Fifteen minutes after this second strike at the World Trade Center, the FAA passed to the NEADS air defenders a report that American Airlines Flight 11 had in fact not crashed; instead, the hijacked aircraft was said to be flying over New Jersey, or even further south, and heading toward Washington, D.C.[22] The confusion over the status of American Flight 11 had begun, however, almost immediately after the North Tower was hit. During the period between the two attacks in New York City, the FAA told the NEADS air defenders that it could not confirm that American Flight 11 had crashed.[23]

4. Less than four minutes before American Airlines Flight 77 crashed into the Pentagon, the FAA told the NEADS air defenders that the flight was missing. The FAA staffer, who did not describe the flight as a hijack, passed the information to the air defenders during a telephone call initiated by NEADS about another problematic aircraft.[24]

5. NEADS personnel were not aware that United Airlines Flight 93 had been hijacked until just over four minutes after it had slammed into an abandoned strip mine in Pennsylvania. Word of United Flight 93's last known latitude and longitude came during a telephone call from an FAA military liaison who was himself unaware that the aircraft had crashed. Twelve minutes after the crash, in the course of a telephone call initiated by NEADS staff, the FAA informed the air defenders that United Flight 93 had gone down at an unknown location northeast of Camp David.[25]

Even a cursory examination of the 9/11 Commission's report and timeline suggests that improving U.S. air defense against any future terrorist attack depends on a quicker FAA determination that a plane has indeed been hijacked and more effective coordination and timely communication between the FAA and the various sectors of NORAD. These enhancements, in fact, have been among the government's critical accomplishments since 9/11, and the success of Operation Noble Eagle has been due in part to improvements in these areas (*see*

Table 1, Timing of FAA Notification to NORAD's Northeast Air Defense Sector, p 54).

Throughout the attacks, and in the hours that followed, military and civilian agencies and leaders endeavored to obtain accurate information, establish interagency communications, and respond in a coordinated way. Their efforts bore increasingly substantial results as the day wore on. But during the critical 109 minutes of the actual attack period, the military response by the U.S. government consisted of the launch by NEADS of four fully armed air defense fighters and a spare jet armed with a 20-mm Gatling gun.[26] None of these aircraft were able to intercept any of the four hijacked planes.[27]

All five fighters launched during the attack period had a single, and the same, potential target: the first aircraft hijacked, American Airlines Flight 11. The first two fighters launched from Otis Air National Guard Base in response to an FAA request for assistance with Flight 11, but it had already crashed by the time the fighters took off.[28] More than thirty-five minutes later, the second three fighters launched from Langley Air Force Base in response to a faulty FAA report that Flight 11 was still aloft and was headed toward Washington, D.C.[29]

The five fighters could not intercept the second, third, or fourth hijacked planes at least in part because NEADS did not ask their pilots to do so. The NEADS air defenders did not ask because they did not know, or knew too late, that United Airlines Flight 175, American Airlines Flight 77, and United Airlines Flight 93 had been hijacked. For their part, FAA air traffic controllers were in most cases unable to expeditiously and accurately determine if and which aircraft were hijacked. Their uncertainties and the resulting delays in notifying the military and requesting assistance were the consequences primarily of the tactics of the hijackers. By murdering the cockpit crews of the four flights, the hijackers rendered the government's antihijacking protocol obsolete; by turning off or altering the flights' transponders, they made locating, tracking, and intercepting the commandeered planes exceedingly difficult.

In almost all pre-9/11 hijackings, the information flow from commercial pilots—under threat but still at the controls—to air traffic controllers, and then, eventually, to NORAD and responding U.S. Air Force pilots, remained intact. Within minutes, the nature of the 9/11 attacks rendered the traditional "hijacking paradigm" invalid.[30] The paradigm assumed that negotiations between hijackers and law enforcement would take place, usually after a commandeered plane landed safely, and that passengers and crew would emerge unscathed. The tactics of the 9/11 hijacker-pilots and their teams took full advantage of these long-held assumptions to keep the victimized passengers and remaining crew under control and the air traffic control system—and, hence, the air defense system—largely in the dark. In a stroke, FAA antihijacking protocols that had been the standard for decades and NORAD air defense response procedures built thereon were outdated and irrelevant. In hindsight and to their credit, many FAA and NEADS employees, with little situational awareness, and often in the ab-

10

sence of senior staff, took the initiative and improvised a response to a catastrophic situation for which they had not trained and were not prepared.[31]

The last hijacking involving coordination between FAA air traffic controllers and management and the U.S. military took place on February 11, 1993, when a twenty-year-old Ethiopian man hijacked Lufthansa Airlines Flight 592 over Austrian airspace shortly after it left Frankfurt International Airport for Cairo and Addis Ababa. Wielding what looked like a semiautomatic pistol but was later found to be a starter's pistol, Nebiu Demeke commandeered the Airbus 310-300 and forced its pilot to divert it to New York after a refueling stop in Hanover, Germany. After the plane landed at John F. Kennedy International Airport, the hijacker surrendered peacefully to the Federal Bureau of Investigation (FBI), ending a nearly twelve-hour ordeal for ninety-four passengers and ten crew members.[32] Notably, four U.S. military servicemen involved in the response to that hijacking played key roles in the air defense response on 9/11.

The commander of the glass-enclosed battle cab overlooking the operations floor at the Northeast Air Defense Sector on 9/11, Col. Robert Marr, was assigned to the NEADS operation section when his commander learned from a news broadcast of the Lufthansa hijacking. Seeking sufficient advance notice for a military response as the aircraft headed toward the United States, Marr told representatives of the Federal Aviation Administration that they needed to pass a request for military assistance up their chain of command. He also alerted his own chain of command to be prepared for such a request. As hours passed, coordination continued at higher levels of authority on the military and FAA sides, and Marr explained the need for an air defense response to the Lufthansa flight during a call he received from the White House. After initially opposing NEADS involvement, the White House called back several hours later that day and authorized the Northeast Air Defense Sector to proceed. The sector scrambled two F–15s from Otis Air National Guard Base, and then two F–16s from Atlantic City Air National Guard Base, to intercept and trail the hijacked aircraft.[33] Marr later recalled, "It took over six hours to gain an initial tail on this occasion."[34]

The lead pilot of the first two fighters sent aloft on 9/11, Lt. Col. Timothy Duffy, had been the second of the two Otis F–15 pilots scrambled in response to the Lufthansa hijacking. After intercepting the errant flight off the coast of eastern Canada, the fighters remained out of sight, about ten miles behind it. They moved within five miles, but above and behind the jet as it neared Kennedy Airport. As it landed, the Otis fighters flew by at low altitude, circled overhead while negotiations proceeded, and then returned to their bases after the hijacker surrendered.[35]

The senior director of the weapons section at the Northeast Air Defense Sector on 9/11, Maj. James Fox, was a NEADS weapons controller during the Lufthansa hijacking. That hijacking, unlike those on 9/11, unfolded during a period of many hours and over a distance of 5,600 miles, and its pilot remained in charge of the cockpit. Thus NEADS personnel were able to receive intelligence far in advance of the aircraft's arrival in U.S. airspace and to prepare for an effective, timely response by reviewing hijack regulations and exercises.[36]

The mission crew commander technician on 9/11, MSgt. Joe McCain, was a NEADS identification technician during the Lufthansa hijacking. His NEADS colleagues gave the flight a "Special 15" classification, as they would Delta Airlines Flight 1989, suspected of being hijacked on September 11, 2001. The Lufthansa hijacking was treated as a law enforcement issue, and the FBI was the lead agency on the ground.[37] Because NEADS personnel exercised for this type of air piracy every week, the Lufthansa hijacking presented in terms of response, according to McCain, a "very easy scenario."[38]

Thanks in part to Marr's initiative, coordination between the FAA and NEADS in response to the Lufthansa hijacking went smoothly. Intercept authorization from higher national authorities came down to NEADS in relative accordance with established interagency procedures, if slowly, and the actual intercept followed known protocols.[39]

U.S. government antihijacking procedures current in 1993 underwent only minor revisions in the years leading up to the 9/11 attacks. Certain high-level instructions and orders in effect on September 11, 2001, set out protocols for FAA-NORAD cooperation and addressed issues surrounding requests for and authorization of military escort aircraft. Two of these official pronouncements laid out procedures to be implemented after the FAA determined that a plane had been hijacked and required military assistance, but they gave no guidance as to how the FAA would decide if a hijacking had, indeed, occurred. That gap was filled, at least in part, by a third order directed to FAA air traffic controllers.

A Chairman of the Joint Chiefs of Staff instruction and attached enclosures dated June 1, 2001, provided guidance and direction to the deputy director for operations, National Military Command Center (NMCC) at the Pentagon; the NORAD commander; and operational commanders for dealing with hijackings of civil or military aircraft. Under the CJCS protocol, which was in effect on September 11, 2001, the head of the Federal Aviation Administration was solely responsible for directing the response of law enforcement agencies to a hijacking. If the FAA administrator decided that law enforcement needed the assistance of the Department of Defense, then he or she would notify, as soon as possible, the NMCC, the "focal point" for any FAA requests for DOD assistance. In this capacity the center would coordinate, on behalf of the DOD, between the FAA and operational commanders. In the event of a hijacking judged to require the assistance of military escort aircraft, the FAA hijack coordinator was to notify the NMCC deputy director of operations, who would contact NEADS or an appropriate unified command to determine the availability of suitable assets and would also forward the FAA request to the secretary of defense for approval. Approvals would return to NMCC for dissemination to NORAD or to the unified command. The center would then authorize direct coordination between the FAA and the designated squadron providing escort aircraft. Normally, NORAD provided such aircraft, in which case the FAA coordinated through the relevant air defense sector.[40]

In an updated special military operations order issued on July 12, 2001, the Federal Aviation Administration set out revised procedures for the escort of hijacked aircraft. It mirrored the protocol described in the CJCS order of June 1 and like the CJCS order, took as its starting point an FAA determination that a confirmed hijacking needed a military escort.[41] The escort would be directed to perform three limited tasks: follow the hijacked aircraft, report anything unusual, and assist search and rescue efforts in the event of an emergency. There was no mention of military aircraft being ordered to shoot down errant planes.[42]

A second FAA order that included a change dated July 12, 2001, set out air traffic control procedures and phraseology applicable to emergencies in general and hijackings in particular. Its provisions were designed for air traffic controllers, who were, in virtually all emergency situations, at the beginning of the decision-making chain, second only to pilots. The order gave them guidance on determining whether an emergency existed, on whether a flight had been hijacked, and on rendering assistance. Controllers were to provide "maximum assistance" to distressed aircraft, and "[e]nlist" the radar, emergency facilities, and services of the military when they deemed them necessary, or at the request of a pilot. But controllers could begin to assist generally only after receiving from pilots certain minimum required information about the nature of the emergency. Instructions on handling hijacked aircraft assumed only one scenario: that their pilots would be able to transmit—"squawk"—to their air traffic controllers a special hijack transponder code, which in September 2001 was Code 7500. On observing this code, a controller was to ask the pilot to verify it; thereafter, the controller was to notify supervisory personnel of the hijack. The controller was also responsible for assisting any military escort aircraft that might eventually be dispatched and to help position them behind the commandeered plane.[43]

Several tragically flawed assumptions about the nature of air piracy underlay CJCS and FAA antihijacking protocols in effect in September 2001. First, nearly all hijackers sought to advance political causes or economic agendas and not their own deaths. Second, hijackers did not go to flight training schools and would not know how to take navigational control of aircraft or make them unidentifiable to air traffic controllers by turning off or altering transponders. Third—this assumption was perhaps the most critical—airline pilots would have the time, opportunity, and ability to notify air traffic controllers, by using a code word over the radio or the special hijack transponder code. Fourth, there would be time for hijack notifications and requests and approvals for military response to pass up and down FAA, NORAD, and DOD chains of command as required.[44]

Even before 9/11, fighter pilots and other military personnel were not entirely sanguine about the prospects of happy outcomes to fighter escorts of hijacked commercial aircraft. The commander of one of the installations that scrambled fighters on September 11, 2001, recalled that military personnel "always joked that . . . [the purpose of a fighter escort of a hijacked aircraft] was plotting the wreckage. . . . you would mark the debris circle."[45]

The effectiveness of the protocols that provided the framework for FAA-NORAD coordination and military air defense in the event of a hijacking relied partly on the actions of the FAA administrator, who determined if a law enforcement response would be sufficient or if DOD assistance would be needed. It also relied heavily on actions that would be taken by the FAA hijack coordinator at FAA headquarters, by personnel at the National Military Command Center, and by the secretary of defense. For various reasons as the 9/11 attacks began, those individuals and entities were unable to facilitate and coordinate FAA-NORAD communications or to authorize and direct air defense operations launched in response.

More fundamentally, however, successful antihijacking protocols and timely air defense response depended on air traffic controllers in FAA air route traffic control centers to determine if a hijack or other emergency situation existed or was imminent. Under standard practices described, air traffic controllers in September 2001 relied largely on notification by pilots to expeditiously confirm a hijack.[46] Indeed, air traffic controllers had been taught in FAA hijack training courses before 9/11 to expect such confirmation.[47] The courses were based on two unalterable beliefs: pilots would remain in control of aircraft during piracy incidents; and they would be able to notify controllers of their situation overtly or covertly from the cockpit in one of three ways: first, by directly confirming verbally that the flight was hijacked;[48] second, by altering the transponder code to the 7500 hijack code, which would cause the word "HIJACK" to flash across the flight's data block on the traffic monitoring unit in the relevant air route traffic control center; or, third, by signaling the air traffic controller with coded language, such as the word "trip" to refer to the course of the aircraft.[49] However, the 9/11 hijackers, having quickly killed or disabled the cockpit crews of all four aircraft, ensured that there would be no such notification.[50] Critically, also, training exercises did not emphasize the FAA and NORAD working together to respond to the extent required on September 11, 2001. While training did afford air traffic controllers the opportunity to practice the pre-9/11 protocol for alerting the military to a hijack threat, it apparently never required them to practice intercept procedures.[51]

Controllers were trained to keep aircraft separated, not to vector them together,[52] and many lacked experience dealing with military aircraft traveling at supersonic speeds.[53] Several controllers on duty during the 9/11 attacks had had air traffic control experience during prior service in the U.S. Air Force, and at least one seasoned veteran believed that his ability to vector a fighter for intercept resulted from his military experience, not from his FAA training.[54] It is unclear whether or not training included a hijack simulation or intercept exercise involving joint FAA-NORAD participation.[55] In any event, training did not prepare controllers for suicide hijackers.[56]

14

The 9/11 Commission determined that, despite this gap in the training of its air traffic controllers, the Federal Aviation Administration had "indeed considered the possibility that terrorists would hijack a plane and use it as a weapon."[57] In the spring of 2001, the agency's intelligence function, the Office of Civil Aviation Security, distributed an unclassified CD-ROM presentation to air carriers and airports, including authorities at Logan, Newark, and Dulles. The briefing, whose overall subject was the increased threat to civil aviation, mentioned the possibility of suicide terrorist hijackings but concluded that "fortunately, we have no indication that any group is currently thinking in that direction."[58] In its *Final Report,* the 9/11 Commission left to an endnote the warning contained in the FAA intelligence presentation: " . . . if a hijacker intended to commit suicide in a spectacular explosion, the terrorist would be likely to prefer a domestic hijacking."[59]

Like air traffic controllers, U.S. commercial airline flight crews and attendants were not trained to confront suicide hijackers. Before 9/11, the airlines' Common Strategy and training, like the FAA's for air traffic controllers, was based on traditional hijacking. In short, as recalled by the "chief pilot" and managing director, Flight Operations Technical for American Airlines, hijackers "were understood to be terrorists that wanted to come out of the thing alive."[60]

Without notification from a pilot, the determination that a flight was hijacked—and not just experiencing serious mechanical difficulties or under the command of an inattentive pilot—rested with the air traffic controller. Absent a "Mayday" or other verbal communication from a pilot, FAA emergency and hijack response protocols directed controllers in doubt about whether or not a situation was an emergency or potential emergency to "handle it as though it were an emergency."[61] Even so, the protocols assumed, in the main, that pilots would be able to communicate and be part of the decision-making process. A controller was to begin determining the type of assistance necessary and rendering it as soon as requests and enough information had been received from the pilot.[62] Even specific instructions on hijacked aircraft were predicated on the notion that the controller would observe the special hijack transponder code, which, it was assumed, would be transmitted by the pilot.[63] In the words of Cleveland Center air traffic controller John Werth, the thirty-year FAA veteran who handled United Airlines Flight 93 on September 11, 2001, "you can't do anything with the aircraft unless he talks to you."[64]

Course deviations, loss of radio contact, and loss or alteration of transponder signals—later determined to be the first signs of trouble on the 9/11 flights—were not unheard of, nor were they necessarily disturbing, particularly if they occurred in isolation. Before the 9/11 attacks, many air traffic controllers had handled commercial aircraft that had gone slightly off course, usually because of weather. A significant course deviation, however, would indicate a serious mechanical problem. Controllers had experience with another notoriously common phenomenon, loss of radio contact with pilots and crew and, much less frequently, with the loss of an aircraft's transponder signal. Before 9/11, controllers would have interpreted the rare instance of simultaneous or nearly simultaneous loss of radio contact and transponder signal as a serious in-flight emergency, one caused by catastrophic equipment failure or a crash, not a hijacking. Likewise, the combination of even a drastic course deviation, loss of radio communications, and loss of transponder could signal an electrical or mechanical failure, not necessarily a hijacking. In any of these circumstances, as on September 11, 2001, the controller would spend several minutes trying to contact the pilot, the airline company, and nearby planes to reestablish communications with the problematic flight and correct its course. Only after those efforts had been tried and failed would the controller raise a more general alarm.[65]

In the event of a hijacking in which the pilot was able to alert a Federal Aviation Administration air route traffic control center, for example by means of the hijack transponder code, the responsible air traffic controller would verify the hijacking with the pilot using the hijack code and then notify his or her supervisor of the incident. To avoid escalating the situation, the controller would not question the pilot but would handle any requests from the cockpit. Routinely, the controller would also clear airspace in front of the hijacked plane.[66] Meanwhile, the supervisor would inform the center's traffic management unit and the operations manager in charge of the incident. Any request for military escort or other assistance would be initiated at the level of the operations manager in charge. The FAA center would then contact the appropriate regional operations center, whose staff would, finally, notify FAA headquarters.[67] There, the hijack coordinator would contact the National Military Command Center to ask for a military escort aircraft, and the center would then seek permission from the Office of the Secretary of Defense to accede to the FAA request. If and when that office approved, it would send the necessary orders down the NORAD chain of command.[68] Thereafter, the NMCC would keep the hijack coordinator abreast of developments. The center would also help FAA air route traffic control centers coordinate directly with and provide tracking information to the North American Aerospace Defense Command.[69] Eventually, an appropriate FAA air traffic controller would assist in discretely placing five miles behind the hijacked aircraft any escort aircraft scrambled in response.[70]

The CJCS instruction and FAA orders, which applied to confirmed hijackings, were bypassed in the emergency air defense response to the attacks of September 11, 2001. The 9/11 Commission maintained that the standard protocol was unsuitable "in every respect" for the occasion.[71] Commissioners were probably correct in concluding that its application that day would not have enhanced the possibilities of intercepting—much less shooting down—the doomed aircraft.[72] But apropos or not, the protocol was by and large not used. That the FAA established direct contact with NEADS, and that NEADS scrambled and launched its alert fighters, had more to do with individual initiative than with adherence to established procedure.

The suicide hijackings launched on September 11, 2001, constituted a type of war unseen on U.S. soil since the Japanese bombing of Pearl Harbor. Like that earlier attack, the success of this "new type of war" was virtually ensured—at least on that day—by its very nature. The strategy and tactics of the four teams of hijackers and the ease with which they and their weapons passed through the aviation security system allowed the perpetrators of the 9/11 attacks to achieve a key element of a successful military campaign—surprise.[73] A number of factors contributed to the fog of war challenging the FAA air traffic control apparatus and the NEADS air defense response system on September 11. Perhaps the primary cause of the resulting tumult was the sine qua non of the 9/11 attacks: the four hijacker-pilots and their shocking synthesis of the tradition of suicide bombing and the tactics of kamikazes.

Much emphasis was placed after the attacks on the fundamentalist motivations of the attackers, but their motivations were relevant in one particular sense: the hijackers and those who inspired and planned the attacks believed they were at war against the financial, commercial, military, and political systems of the West. But their motivations were irrelevant in at least one respect: the U.S. federal government and the national aviation and air defense systems were in many ways ill prepared to respond quickly and effectively to a surprise attack launched from within the country by attackers of any motivation.

In the end, three of the four hijacked flights reached their targets; the fourth, United Airlines Flight 93, whose hijackers probably intended to hit the Capitol, failed to do so because of unexpected timing and human endeavor (*see* Table 2, General Overview of the Four Hijacked Flights, p 55). The fourth attack was thwarted, in part because of the flight's tardy takeoff and a late takeover by the hijackers. The delays gave passengers time to learn from loved ones on the ground of the other hijackings, to face their own probable fate, and to collectively try to retake the aircraft.

This heroic civilian counterattack was not the only effort undertaken on the morning of September 11, 2001, to defend the country against the hijacked aircraft-turned-guided-missiles. As the attacks unfolded in an increasingly chaotic and deadly situation, FAA air traffic controllers and NEADS air defense personnel raced to obtain timely, accurate, comprehensible, and actionable information, and to prepare, launch, and direct an aerial counterattack with the small force of available alert aircraft.

During several decades of traditional hijackings, the expeditious launch of NORAD air defense fighters depended largely on timely hijack notification by the Federal Aviation Administration, which in turn depended on how quickly FAA air traffic controllers determined that a flight was hijacked, which in its turn depended on maintaining ground communications with a hijacked plane and, particularly, on the ability of a victimized pilot to notify controllers of his or her predicament. The 9/11 hijackers were in no way traditional, however. They swiftly murdered the pilots, took over flight control of the airliners, ceased responding to direction from air traffic controllers, changed course, and turned off or altered transponders. The four teams of hijackers undertook some of these actions in different sequences, but the result was the same: in a matter of minutes, the traditional communication chain, from pilot to FAA to NORAD, was shattered; determining a hijack became highly problematic; and traditional air defense response protocols were rendered obsolete. What remained to be reconstituted, indeed, established, was an effective communications link between the FAA and NORAD or specifically, on September 11, 2001, its Northeast Air Defense Sector.

American Airlines Flight 11

The Federal Aviation Administration notified NEADS of the first hijacking—later determined to be American Airlines Flight 11—just under nine minutes before the plane slammed into the north tower of the World Trade Center. This was the longest notice NEADS air defenders received that day.[74] That circumstance, and other aspects of the first attack, make the hijacking of Flight 11 and the sequence and development of the air traffic control-air defense response of particular interest.

American Airlines Flight 11, a Boeing 767-223,[75] scheduled to depart Boston Logan International Airport at 7:45 a.m. EDT on a nonstop flight to Los Angeles International Airport, pushed back from the gate at 7:40 a.m. and lifted off at 7:59 a.m. On board were a pilot, first officer, nine flight attendants, and eighty-one passengers, including five al Qaeda terrorists.[76] Just under fourteen minutes into the flight, in its last routine communication, the cockpit crew acknowledged navigational instructions[77] from air traffic control specialist Peter Zalewski, on duty in Area C at FAA's Boston Air Route Traffic Control Center, Nashua, New Hampshire. Sixteen seconds into the transmission, Zalewski instructed the pilots to climb to 35,000 feet. They did not acknowledge his direction or the controller's subsequent radio transmissions. Investigators, including the 9/11 Commission, later concluded that the hijacking occurred at that point in the flight, but Boston Center personnel did not suspect for approximately ten more minutes that American Airlines Flight 11 had been hijacked (*see* Table 3, American Airlines Flight 11 and 9/11 Commission Timeline, p 56).[78]

Becoming increasingly concerned as the plane began moving into the arrival route for Boston Logan Airport and approaching another sector's airspace, Zalewski checked his own radio equipment, which was working properly; tried to contact the flight on an emergency frequency;[79] checked the frequency used by Boston Approach, the previous sector; and tried to contact American Airlines through the Aeronautical Radio Incorporated (ARINC) system. Thinking that the plane might be having an electrical problem, he reported to his supervisor, Jon Schippani, the sole operational supervisor in charge of Area C that day, and they began to follow procedures for handling a "no radio" (NORDO) aircraft.[80] At that time, neither suspected a hijacking.[81]

Over the next few minutes, Zalewski and other Boston Center air traffic controllers and radar associates attempted to contact American Airlines Flight 11 several times by various methods on different frequencies, enlisting help from the previous sector, Boston Approach, and also from other American aircraft. American Airlines Flight 11 did not respond.[82] Soon thereafter, as the situation escalated during what would be the missing aircraft's last six or seven minutes of flight, John Hartling, Zalewski's colleague and a former U.S. Air Force air traffic controller, expanded the center's search for assistance by contacting U.S. Air Flight 583 and United Airlines Flight 175. These flights succeeded in achieving visual contact with the hijacked plane and identified its altitude as between 27,000 and 29,000 feet. United Flight 175 would soon, itself, be hijacked.[83]

In the midst of these early and ongoing efforts by Boston Center personnel to communicate with American Airlines Flight 11 and to direct other aircraft away from its path, one of the hijackers in the cockpit of the aircraft turned off its transponder.[84] With the loss of this secondary radar return, the plane's flight data tag indicating its speed, altitude, airline identification, and flight number instantly disappeared from Boston Center radar scope displays. American Airlines Flight 11 was thereafter observed as only a primary radar target, a simple blip, by Zalewski and other controllers when they switched their computers to display primary targets.[85] They were able to continue to track the flight after giving it a data tag.[86] Without that tag, the blip of American Airlines Flight 11 would have been indistinguishable from the sea of blips, visible on FAA and NEADS scopes, representing thousands of airplanes in U.S. airspace that morning.[87]

The disabling or alteration of the transponders on all four aircraft hijacked on September 11, 2001, was intentional and calculated by the hijackers and had serious consequences for FAA and NEADS personnel attempting to find, track, and intercept the missing planes. Without properly operating transponders to respond to queries from their ground-based radar, FAA air traffic controllers could not easily identify and track the primary-only flights. Critically, controllers could not determine the planes' altitude without the help of a pilot flying nearby who might be able, at best, to provide estimates; nor could they easily determine the planes' latitude or longitude coordinates.[88] Unfortunately, most Boston Center personnel did not know that NEADS air defense scope operators could determine altitude on nontransponding, primary-only aircraft. However, several key individuals at Boston Center—notably, its military operations specialist, Colin Scoggins—did know and realized that this capability would be another reason to contact the military, in addition to asking for fighters to escort or tail a hijacked aircraft. At the New York Air Route Traffic Control Center, at Ronkonkoma, on Long Island in New York, controllers also knew that they could not determine altitude on a plane that was on only primary radar. But some key staffers there, including twenty-year FAA veteran Kevin Delaney, the supervisor of New York Center's quality assurance office on 9/11, did not know that the military could do so.[89] To successfully find any airplane in the sky, the Northeast Air Defense Sector needed to know either the plane's transponder code—Mode 3 in military parlance and Mode C in FAA parlance—or the plane's latitude and longitude coordinates.[90]

At that point on September 11, the loss of a transponder on a commercial aircraft did not mean that it had been hijacked. However, Zalewski and his colleagues were even more concerned that the aircraft was having serious electrical or mechanical trouble. Still, no one at Boston Center yet suspected that the plane had been hijacked. Their views soon changed dramatically. Just over ten minutes after the aircraft's last routine communication, Zalewski heard two clicks over the frequency assigned to several planes in the sector, including American Airlines Flight 11.[91] He then heard what his experience in international air traffic control told him was a Middle Eastern voice transmitting the following radio message:[92] "[W]e have some planes[.] [J]ust stay quiet[,] and you'll be okay[.] [W]e are returning to the airport."[93]

The transmission was garbled, and Zalewski could not decipher the first sentence.[94] Seconds after receiving this transmission, he clearly heard a second threatening transmission, which convinced him that the flight had been hijacked. An unidentified voice—probably that of Mohammed Atta—from the cockpit of what was subsequently determined to be American Airlines Flight 11 made the following transmission at 8:24:56 a.m. EDT: "[N]obody move[.] [E]verything will be okay[.] [I]f you try to make any moves[,] you'll endanger yourself and the airplane[.] [J]ust stay quiet[.]"[95] A little over a minute later, near Albany, New York, the flight began a hard but level left turn to the south.[96] A third transmission came at 8:33:59 a.m. EDT: "[N]obody move please[.] [W]e are going back to the airport[.] [D]on't try to make any stupid moves[.]"[97]

The importance of these transmissions to the recognition of American Airlines Flight 11 as hijacked, and, thus, to the air defense response, cannot be overstated. The 9/11 Commission believed that the hijackers intended to broadcast these messages to the passengers over the cabin's public address channel.[98] It seems likely that Atta wanted to keep the passengers quiet, seated, and unaware of their approaching fate. The first two of the three threatening communications came less than two minutes before Atta made a major course alteration to begin the southbound turn. The third transmission came about three minutes before American Airlines Flight 11 began its steep and final descent from 29,000 feet and less than thirteen minutes before it crashed into the North Tower.[99]

The hijackers' announcements, however, were not made over the public address system and so were not heard by anyone on board American Airlines Flight 11.[100] That the transmissions were heard, instead, by air traffic controllers and by other planes on the same frequency suggests that the hijackers pushed the wrong button, not knowing how to properly operate available communications systems.[101] Included in the group of planes on the same frequency, ironically, was United Airlines Flight 175. That flight's captain and first officer—to avoid being overheard on the frequency by anyone doing harm in the cockpit of American Airlines Flight 11—waited more than fifteen minutes, until they were passed out of Boston Center airspace, to tell David Bottiglia at the New York Air Route Traffic Control Center that they had heard "a suspicious transmission" after departing Boston Logan.[102]

After receiving the second transmission, Zalewski put the communications from American Airlines Flight 11 on the overhead microphone so that the entire section could hear what was going on. Because he had not clearly understood the first sentence of the garbled transmission, he asked Boston Center quality assurance specialist Robert Jones to pull the audio tapes so that the transmission could be analyzed.[103] Some minutes later, as soon as he had reviewed the first communication, Jones told Terry Biggio, the operations manager in charge at Boston Center, that a speaker with what was clearly a Middle Eastern accent had begun the transmission with the following statement: "We have some planes." Biggio, in turn, immediately—ironically, seconds before United Airlines Flight 175 crashed into 2 World Trade Center—passed this information to the New England Regional Operations Center (ROC) in Burlington, Massachusetts. He did not call the Washington Operations Center (WOC) directly to inform FAA headquarters of the hijacking, but he joined an ROC conference call that he believed was actively monitored by WOC personnel.[104]

In the meantime, the second threatening transmission had convinced Boston Center personnel that American Airlines Flight 11 had been hijacked. In Biggio's view, the combination of the loss of radio contact, the loss of the transponder, and the course deviation was serious and made it necessary to contact the Regional Operations Center. But he later doubted that Boston Center personnel would have concluded that the plane had been hijacked had they not heard the threatening communications from the cockpit.[105]

At that point, eleven minutes after the last routine communication from Flight 11, Boston Center air traffic controllers and managers realized that the aircraft had been hijacked. However, Boston Center would not notify the air defenders at the Northeast Air Defense Sector for another twelve minutes. The pre-9/11 "conceptual box," which circumscribed FAA and NORAD antihijacking protocols, planning, and practice, remained in place even longer.[106] It was based on two premises regarding commercial aviation and hijacking, and by extension, national defense: pilots would remain at the controls of their planes and would be able to communicate their predicament to air traffic controllers; and hijackers did not know how to fly planes and did not want to die. The first major hijacking of the twenty-first century rendered both notions obsolete.

The pre-9/11 conceptual box limited the ability of FAA and NORAD personnel to predict or even imagine what could happen in the cockpit of a hijacked aircraft. Consequently, many Boston Center personnel believed that the threatening transmissions were being made by one or more individuals in the background of the flight deck. They also believed that some other individual, probably the American Airlines Flight 11 pilot, was intentionally and surreptitiously keying a push-to-talk button on the aircraft's yoke to allow air traffic controllers to hear what was going on in the cockpit.[107] This confusing and faulty assumption—that the American Airlines pilot remained at the helm for much of the flight—resurfaced throughout the morning in official FAA headquarters and regional operations center records[108] despite widespread awareness that at least one person on board had been stabbed, that communications with the aircraft had been lost, and that its altitude had been fluctuating.[109] A New England Regional Operations Center daily log even noted a report that not only was the pilot keying the microphone, the *crew* of the hijacked aircraft had turned the transponder off.[110] The belief that the American Airlines pilot was keying the microphone was reported as fact by major newspapers in the days after the attacks[111] and was repeated two years later to 9/11 Commission staff by at least one Boston Center supervisor.[112] In fact, however, after the attacks, the FBI reviewed the speech patterns and other characteristics of the recorded transmissions, and its analyst concluded definitively—as Zalewski and Jones had surmised that day—that one of the hijackers in the cockpit made the transmissions, speaking directly into the microphone.[113]

The notion that airline pilots always remained at the controls of hijacked aircraft persisted beyond the demise of American Airlines Flight 11. At the Northeast Air Defense Sector, seconds after learning that FAA personnel were dealing with a possible second hijacking, that of United Airlines Flight 175, NEADS personnel in the surveillance section remarked on the absence of the "7500" hijack transponder code signal from its cockpit crew: "We have smart terrorists today, their [sic] not giving them [the pilots] a chance to squawk[.]"[114]

The conceptual box also limited the framework in which hijacking was interpreted. Before 9/11, a hijack was thought to entail a diversion to Cuba or a ransom demand and was not considered an act of terrorism.[115] The threatening communications convinced Boston Center controllers and managers that American Airlines Flight 11 had indeed been hijacked. But most of them—and, soon, their opposite numbers at New York Air Route Traffic Control Center—believed that the plane might land at Kennedy Airport or even Albany Airport,[116] or would head to Cuba or elsewhere in the Caribbean.[117] No one seriously considered any other outcome.[118] Even in the later stages of the flight's path, as New York Center controllers watched it head toward Kennedy Airport until it disappeared from their scopes, some believed that its failure to reappear on screen was due to malfunctioning radar. In the absence of any information that what had hit the North Tower was in fact American Airlines Flight 11, some controllers initially thought that the aircraft might have landed at Kennedy.[119]

Just after Boston Center received the second transmission, and in accordance with FAA-NORAD protocol, center managers and controllers notified colleagues and superiors across the organizational structure and up the command chain of the FAA that a suspected hijack was in progress. Daniel L. Bueno, the supervisory traffic management coordinator, and Terry Biggio, the operations manager in charge, notified the New England Regional Operations Center and the Air Traffic Control System Command Center in Herndon, Virginia, both of which were in contact shortly thereafter with the Washington Operations Center at FAA headquarters. Bueno and Biggio and several Boston Center controllers also began coordinating with New York Center, New York TRACON (Terminal Radar Approach Control) in Westbury, and Washington and Cleveland Air Route Traffic Control Centers.[120] Despite these endeavors, notable gaps in communication and coordination soon appeared. For example, a teleconference that Bueno established at the suggestion of Herndon Command Center between Boston, New York, and Cleveland Centers did not include Indianapolis Center. There was no indication that the hijacked plane would head toward Indianapolis Center's airspace, and, thus, no reason to distract its controllers.[121] More significant at this point was that "FAA headquarters began to follow the hijack protocol but did not contact the NMCC to request a fighter escort."[122]

The situation with American Airlines Flight 11 began to deteriorate quickly after Zalewski received the second threatening transmission. A few minutes after the flight turned to the south, Boston Center personnel, lacking precise information on its altitude, were particularly concerned when they discerned a decrease in the speed of its data tag. Bueno and the military operations specialist, Colin Scoggins, believed that this loss of speed meant the plane was possibly descending.[123] Just after Zalewski and his section colleagues heard the third threatening transmission, and in conjunction with ongoing efforts to alert the FAA chain of command to the possible hijacking, several center staffers launched a parallel, two-part effort, on their own initiative and outside the bonds of protocol, to notify the military and expedite the air defense side of the hijacking response equation.

The first part of the effort began at 8:34 a.m. EDT when Bueno called Cape TRACON, an FAA facility at Otis Air National Guard Base at Falmouth, on Cape Cod, in Massachusetts. Because of his experience with a scramble to escort a hijacked aircraft in the early 1980s, Bueno was aware that military assistance came from Otis.[124] He knew that an FAA letter of agreement with Cape TRACON set out the procedure for active fighter scrambles, under which his call should have gone to the Northeast Air Defense Sector. But he called Cape TRACON directly because of the urgency of the situation, because the facility was the FAA contact point for Otis,[125] and possibly because he may not have been sure how to contact Otis himself.[126] Bueno spoke first with a Cape TRACON air traffic controller, Steven Walsh, and then immediately thereafter with Tim Spence, the operational supervisor, about contacting Otis to request that fighters be scrambled to "go tail" American Airlines Flight 11. Bueno told Spence that the flight was "a possible hijack," and Spence assured Bueno several times that he would pass the request to Otis.[127] At the same time, Walsh heard the Cape TRACON flight data specialist say that he was trying to telephone the command post at Otis.[128] On September 11, 2001, the North American Aerospace Defense

Command had limited assets; under its control were only fourteen fighters on air defense alert, two each at seven alert sites in the United States. Two of these, Otis Air National Guard Base and Langley Air Force Base, were force providers for the mission of the Northeast Air Defense Sector. The Otis facility, home to the 102d Fighter Wing, was the only air defense base on the East Coast between Washington, D.C., and the Canadian border.[129] Bueno apparently also made an additional phone call or calls. Years after the 9/11 attacks, he told author Lynn Spencer that he called the Otis Tower. A controller there told him to contact the Northeast Air Defense Sector, the only authority that could order a scramble.[130] Scoggins, Bueno's colleague, recalled just over a week after the attacks that Bueno had called the 102d Fighter Wing and was told that the wing "needed a scramble order over the scramble circuit."[131]

The second part of Dan Bueno's effort to scramble fighters began concurrently with or immediately after his conversation with Spence. Over the next several minutes, at least two of Bueno's Boston Center coworkers, independently or at his direction, tried to contact the Northeast Air Defense Sector directly. After the American Airlines Flight 11 situation began to escalate, William Dean, then working as John Hartling's radar associate in Area E, Sector 20, left his position and reported to the Traffic Management Unit watch desk. There he made several calls, including to NEADS, where, he thought, there might be air defense fighters. Dean expected that a quick and effective procedure to get military assistance existed. He found, instead, that the information flow between the FAA and NEADS was "muddled."[132] In addition, Bueno asked Joseph Cooper, a colleague in the Traffic Management Unit, to call the military for assistance. Cooper reached TSgt. Jeremy W. Powell, on the operations floor as a NEADS senior director (weapons) technician, at 8:37:24 a.m.:

> *Boston Center (Cooper):* Hi. Boston Center TMU [Traffic Management Unit]. We have a problem here. We have a hijacked aircraft headed towards New York, and we need you guys to—we need someone to scramble some F–16s or something up there, help us out.
>
> *NEADS (Powell):* Is this real world or exercise?
>
> *Boston Center (Cooper):* No, this is not an exercise, not a test.[133]

Cooper did not know that any military exercises were planned for September 11, 2001. However, NEADS personnel were indeed expecting a planned exercise, Vigilant Guardian, to begin at 9:00 a.m. EDT,[134] but it was on hold because of a Russian Bear exercise.[135] Because of Vigilant Guardian, the battle cab was already staffed and concluding a briefing on the exercise.[136] Powell's question would be repeated a number of times that morning by his colleagues and superiors, who initially wondered—as Powell had done—if the details they heard over the next few minutes of the suspected hijacking might actually be simulated scenarios that planners were inserting into the training exercise.[137] Even after the crash of United Airlines Flight 175, NEADS air defenders continued to emphasize the "real-" or "live-world" nature of the morning's events and to alert others that they were not part of the previously planned exercise.[138]

Powell contacted Maj. Dawne L. Deskins, who was then in the battle cab as the NEADS aircraft control and warning officer for the Vigilant Guardian exercise. When she arrived on the operations floor, she confirmed with Powell that the call from Boston Center involved a real-world hijack, and Powell put her on the phone.[139] Cooper explained to her, in greater detail, the situation and his request for assistance, although he did not realize that the alert fighters at Otis were F–15s and not F–16s:

> *Boston Center (Cooper):* We have a hijacked aircraft headed towards the New York metro area, wondering if you could, umm, send someone up there. Some F–16s maybe out of Otis[.]
>
> *NEADS (Deskins):* Okay, do you have a Mode 3 on it[?]
> . . .
> *Boston Center (Cooper):* Nope, it is just a primary target only . . . [W]e lost the . . . Mode C on it, so you would have to get up in the air[,] and we would have to vector you towards the aircraft[.]
> . . .
> *NEADS (Deskins):* . . . Can you give us a lat.lon. [latitude-longitude] where you think he is . . . [?]
>
> *Boston Center (Cooper):* Yeah, hold on a second . . . [140]

Boston Center was still tracking the errant flight's primary radar return, but because the transponder signal was lost, the center would have to control the intercept until NEADS identification technicians could find the aircraft. Without the transponder signal and, therefore, without a radar point, NEADS personnel needed the plane's latitude and longitude coordinates.[141] Within minutes, these exchanges between Boston Center and NEADS personnel would lead to the placing on battle stations and, shortly thereafter, the scrambling of two F–15 fighters from Otis Air National Guard Base.

After his conversation with Dan Bueno at Boston Center, Tim Spence at Cape TRACON began his telephone calls by contacting the Otis Air National Guard Base Tower to alert personnel there of the American Airlines Flight 11 situation and to ask how to facilitate Bueno's request for fighters.[142] Otis Tower personnel gave Spence a telephone number for the Otis base operations desk and/or the Otis supervisor of flying desk and apparently also told him that a scramble

An image of the crash of American Airlines Flight 77 into the Pentagon, captured by a facility security camera.

A gray smoke plume rising above the crash site of United Airlines Flight 93 near Shanksville, Pennsylvania. Photo, "End of Serenity," used with permission of Valencia McClatchey, photographer and copyright owner.

The Pentagon in flames, minutes after the crash of American Airlines Flight 77. Foam residue is visible on the building's facade, before its collapse. Unattributed DOD photo.

Rubble at Ground Zero, September 19, 2001, one week after al Qaeda terrorists flew American Airlines Flight 11 and United Airlines Flight 175 into the World Trade Center towers, causing their collapse. U.S. Navy photo by Photographer's Mate 2d Class Aaron Peterson.

F–16s of the 119th Fighter Wing, North Dakota Air National Guard, flying a combat air patrol over the Pentagon and Washington, D.C., as part of Operation Noble Eagle, November 2001. Air National Guard photo.

An F–15 of the 102d Fighter Wing, Massachusetts Air National Guard, flying over lower Manhattan and Ground Zero during an Operation Noble Eagle combat air patrol mission several months after the 9/11 attacks. Air National Guard photo by Lt. Col. Bill "Torch" Ramsey.

An F–16 Fighting Falcon flying over the Pentagon as part of Operation Noble Eagle, September 24, 2003. The aircraft is assigned to the 20th Fighter Wing at Shaw Air Force Base, South Carolina. U.S. Air Force photo by SSgt. Aaron D. Allmon II.

Two F–16 Fighting Falcons flying over San Francisco Bay and into precontact position with a KC–135E Stratotanker before refueling during an Operation Noble Eagle training patrol, March 16, 2004. The F–16s are with the California Air National Guard's 144th Fighter Wing in Fresno. The KC–135 is with the 940th Aerial Refueling Wing at Beale Air Force Base, California. U.S. Air Force photo by MSgt. Lance Cheung.

required authorization from the Northeast Air Defense Sector. Spence then called the base operations building and told personnel there of the possible hijacking. Spence acknowledged that he did not have authority to order a fighter scramble, but he advised the operations desk to prepare to receive a scramble order.[143]

At this point, the lines of communication and hijack notification between Cape TRACON, Otis Tower, and Otis base operations become less clear. Otis Tower personnel apparently also called the operations building and spoke with TSgt. Margie Woody, who transferred the tower's call to TSgt. Michael Kelly.[144] As the full-time technician in the Command Post, Kelly was responsible for communicating NORAD and NEADS directives to Otis Air National Guard Base. Kelly recalled that he gave the caller, who he identified as Boston Center—not Otis Tower—the NEADS number and also transferred the call.[145] The caller may in fact have been neither Boston Center nor Otis Tower, but instead, Cape TRACON: Spence later recalled that by the time he spoke with a male military staffer at the Northeast Air Defense Sector, Boston Center had already contacted the NEADS air defenders.[146] Kelly then called the supervisor of flying desk and notified Lt. Col. Jonathan T. "Tracer" Treacy, the commander of the 102d Fighter Wing's 101st Fighter Squadron and the supervisor of flying for the day.[147] Kelly also called NEADS personnel, to notify them of the possible hijacking and scramble request. He reached MSgt. Joe McCain at the mission crew commander technician console position, who already knew of the hijacking because less than a minute before, Joseph Cooper had spoken with TSgt. Jeremy Powell, and the NEADS response to the hijack notification and scramble request had already begun.[148]

Although they were not discussed in the 9/11 Commission *Final Report*, the calls placed by Spence and by Otis Tower personnel to the operations desk helped expedite the response of the two Otis air alert fighter pilots to the order to battle stations placed by NEADS personnel at 8:41 a.m. EDT.[149] Spence did not know it at the time, but he speculated later that the alert pilot had "some degree of warning" of the approaching scramble order because he may have been at the desk when Spence called Otis Air National Guard Base.[150] Lt. Col. Timothy Duffy, the 101st Fighter Squadron's director of operations and one of two alert pilots at Otis on the morning of September 11, was in fact near the break room near the operations desk. On duty there was MSgt. Mark Rose, who received a call from Otis Tower relaying news from Boston Center about a possible hijacking. Rose, the superintendent of aviation management, alerted Duffy, and then the call was redirected to Kelly at the Command Post.[151]

A traditional Guardsman and a pilot for a major airline, Duffy was disappointed to be on alert instead of on the flying schedule during the morning of September 11. As the operations officer, in charge of training, Duffy always warned his colleagues to be careful as they headed out for their training assignments. About ten minutes before his exchange with Rose, Duffy later recalled, one of his coworkers had commented on the date—9/11—and had said, "'Hey, it's a 911 day.' You know, dial 911. Everybody be careful, not even knowing [, yet, about the hijacking]. . . ."[152]

Duffy did not take the news from Rose of a suspected hijacking lightly, recalling later, "in an ASA [air sovereignty alert] squadron, that is not one of those words you throw around." In addition, Otis fighters were on five-minute alert. Although the squadron could not take orders from the FAA, Duffy hoped to get ready while awaiting NEADS instructions and the expected call to battle stations. He, therefore, radioed his fellow alert pilot to suit up.[153]

On alert duty with Duffy, covering the shift for another pilot flying a training mission that morning, was full-time Guardsman Maj. Daniel S. "Nasty" Nash. Listed as lead in the alert roster, Nash was in his office when he received instructions to suit up from Duffy. He learned of the possible hijacking when he reported to the locker room, where Duffy was already suiting up. After hearing of Duffy's prior hijacking experience, Nash told him to take the lead on the expected scramble.[154] Duffy stopped in the Command Post to tell Lieutenant Colonel Treacy that he and Nash were swapping leads. Treacy, meanwhile, had telephoned the Northeast Air Defense Sector to report the FAA scramble request. The NEADS commander, Col. Robert Marr, would have authority to scramble the fighters. By then, Joseph Cooper at Boston Center had spoken with TSgt. Jeremy Powell at NEADS.[155] Treacy was on two telephones, one to FAA personnel and the other to NEADS personnel, and he was "trying to get them to talk to each other." Treacy put the phones down and told Duffy that the hijacked aircraft was a 767, en route from Boston to California, and he may also have identified the plane as American Airlines Flight 11.[156]

Duffy then joined Nash—who at that point knew only that they were responding to a possible hijacking—as they headed to a Ford pickup and drove to the alert barn. Along the way, they heard Kelly pass along an order from the Northeast Air Defense Sector by sounding the klaxon to alert all personnel to go to their battle stations.[157] As Duffy later recalled,

> we went out and hopped in the alert vehicle and were driving out there. We . . . [were] going like 80 [mph]—it's only about one-half mile. . . . We were half way there, and we hear "Alpha Kilo one two, battle stations." Which is good, because now [that order is] . . . coming from NEADS. So, we are no longer doing phone calls from Boston Center to Otis Tower to the squadron, which is the way I got notified.

Duffy and Nash, having saved several minutes' time by suiting up before receiving the order to battle stations, then hopped into their jets, strapped in, and waited for further orders. Duffy had time to tell his crew chief, SMSgt. Wing K. Ng, waiting at the bottom of his ladder, that there was a suspected hijacking of a 767 out of Boston.[158]

As these details reveal, after determining that American Airlines Flight 11 was a possible hijack, FAA air traffic control staff at the Boston Air Route Traffic Control Center launched two efforts, in parallel lines of communication to Otis Air National Guard Base and to the Northeast Air Defense Sector, to try to get fighters scrambled.[159] Boston Center's telephone calls to Otis helped expedite the response of the two air alert pilots on duty at the base on the morning of September 11. This hijack notification and request for fighter assistance—which passed from FAA personnel directly to Air Force personnel and outside the prescribed antihijacking protocol—enabled Duffy and Nash to suit up and head toward their fighters in advance of a NEADS order to battle stations.[160]

Meanwhile, in Rome, New York, NEADS battle commander Colonel Marr learned from a subordinate of Boston Center's call and its scramble request. Confirming that the hijacking was "real world" and not part of the morning's Vigilant Guardian exercise, Marr put the Otis fighters on battle stations. Doing so, he recalled later, saved "about three minutes from the scramble time."[161]

Marr then informed the Continental U.S. Region of NORAD of the possible hijacking. He reached CONR headquarters at Tyndall Air Force Base, Florida, and spoke first with Lt. Col. Randy "Cat" Morris, the deputy director of fighter operations. Referring to his decision to place the two Otis air alert fighters at battle stations, Marr told Morris about the FAA request for assistance and indicated that "NEADS was 'forward leaning' fighters from Otis." After speaking with Marr, Morris directed that the Vigilant Guardian exercise be suspended.[162] Morris later recalled that "The CONR staff had no real[-]time situational awareness." They received information on 9/11 from several sources, including multiple chat channels and secure telephones, CNN, and the three CONR sectors.[163]

Shortly thereafter, Marr spoke with Maj. Gen. Larry K. Arnold, the First Air Force and CONR commander, and told him of these developments.[164] Marr sought and received Arnold's authorization to scramble the fighters to intercept the hijacked aircraft. Both men were well aware, as Morris had pointed out to Marr, that hijacking was considered a law enforcement issue, and they realized that a number of notifications and clearances—from the FAA to the National Military Command Center and all the way up to the Office of the Secretary of Defense—were required under the federal government's antihijacking protocol before a scramble could be launched. But Arnold decided that the scramble should proceed and that they would "get permission later." Arnold later recalled, "We didn't wait for that. We scrambled the aircraft, told them get airborne, and we would seek clearances later."[165]

Because Arnold, Marr, and the NEADS air defenders did not know the precise location of American Airlines Flight 11, Arnold authorized Marr to scramble the two Otis F–15s toward Warning Area 105, also known as Whiskey 105.[166] This military-controlled airspace extended over an area of the Atlantic Ocean south of Martha's Vineyard and covered nearly to New York City.[167]

Arnold and Marr intended to keep the Otis fighters in Whiskey 105 while staff obtained further information on the track of the hijacked aircraft.[168] In Arnold's view, the scramble would be conducted in cooperation with the FAA, and "the only order the pilots had from CONR was to hold over the water until further directed."[169] However, Marr believed, in the circumstances prevailing that morning and without knowing the location of the hijacked plane, that the NEADS mission crew commander, Maj. Kevin Nasypany, had "the discretion to take the Otis fighters directly to New York City."[170]

After their conversation, Marr passed the order directing the flight of the two Otis F–15s to scramble to Nasypany,[171] and Arnold called NORAD. The NORAD battle staff was in place at Cheyenne Mountain Operations Center (CMOC) because of the Vigilant Guardian exercise and NORAD's Operation Northern Denial. Arnold later recalled that he spoke with an unnamed deputy commander for operations,[172] who told the CONR commander to proceed with the scramble and said that NORAD staff would contact the Pentagon—specifically, the National Military Command Center—to get the clearances. Arnold apparently also spoke with Maj. Gen. Eric A. Findley, Canadian Forces, the CMOC battle staff director and NORAD director of operations to facilitate getting the clearances.[173] In accordance with NORAD procedures,[174] Findley contacted NORAD commander Gen. Ralph E. Eberhart.[175]

Minutes after Nasypany's scramble order, and as Duffy and Nash were preparing to take off, Boston Center reported to NEADS personnel that a plane, possibly a 737, had crashed into the World Trade Center. Nasypany realized that the report was unconfirmed and might be inaccurate but also that the destroyed aircraft might be American Airlines Flight 11. Noting that the flight's last reported position was south of John F. Kennedy Airport, Nasypany directed his staff to continue to work with FAA air traffic controllers to clear the Otis F–15s to the New York City area.[176]

The Otis fighters, designated Panta 45 and 46, were airborne at 8:52 a.m. EDT.[177] Unbeknownst to the pilots, their target, American Airlines Flight 11, had crashed into the north tower of the World Trade Center six minutes earlier, at 8:46:25 EDT, less than a minute after Duffy and Nash had received the scramble order.[178] Nash later recalled that he and Duffy "were up even before the jets' radar kicked in."[179] Nasypany and the NEADS air defenders initially headed them over water toward New York City. "[T]he original flight strip for the fighters gave a destination of Kennedy Airport."[180] The Otis fighters headed northeast, the fastest route from the runway, made a tight turn, and headed toward their assigned vector.[181]

Just over three minutes into their flight, Duffy learned from Boston Center, Cape Sector, that American Airlines Flight 11 had crashed into the World Trade Center. Its demise suddenly called into question the Panta flight's mission. Duffy consulted with NEADS personnel, who told him, "the mission is holding."[182] Nasypany, on a phone with Marr in the battle cab, quickly determined that the Panta flight should—in the absence now of any target and to avoid heavily congested civilian airspace in the New York area—proceed to Whiskey 105 and remain in a holding pattern, at an altitude to be chosen by Boston Center, south of the Long Island coast.[183]

The upper stories of the North Tower were on fire, but the attack on the United States was not over. Unbeknownst to Boston Center, Duffy, Nash, and NEADS and CONR personnel, including Marr, Nasypany, and Arnold, another commandeered plane, in its final two minutes of flight, was bearing down on the south tower of the World Trade Center. Within minutes, the mission of the Otis fighters would change from holding in military airspace off Long Island to flying over Manhattan.

United Airlines Flight 175

The Federal Aviation Administration notified the Northeast Air Defense Sector of a "second possible hijack" almost simultaneously with the crash of United Airlines Flight 175 into the South Tower.[184] United Airlines Flight 175, a Boeing 767-222,[185] was scheduled to depart Boston Logan International Airport at 8:00 a.m. EDT on a nonstop flight to Los Angeles International Airport. It pushed back from the gate at 7:58 a.m. and lifted off at 8:14 a.m., at roughly the same moment that the hijackers on board American Airlines Flight 11 were launching their attack. On board United Flight 175 were a pilot, first officer, seven flight attendants, and fifty-six passengers, including five al Qaeda terrorists.[186] Twenty-four minutes into the flight, the cockpit crew responded in the affirmative to air traffic controller David Bottiglia at New York Air Route Traffic Control Center, at Ronkonkoma, on Long Island, who had asked if they had spotted American Airlines Flight 11. Bottiglia, as it happened, was assigned to both aircraft that morning. Twenty-eight minutes into the flight, in their last routine communication with Bottiglia, the cockpit crew members of United Flight 175 completed their report on the "suspicious transmission" from an unidentified plane that they had heard shortly after departing Boston. This was later determined to have been Atta's first announcement from the cockpit of American Airlines Flight 11. Investigators, including the 9/11 Commission, later concluded that the hijackers aboard United Flight 175 probably launched their assault only seconds after the communication with Bottiglia, sometime between 8:42 and 8:46 a.m. EDT (*see* Table 4, United Airlines Flight 175 and 9/11 Commission Timeline, p 57).[187]

The first signs of trouble on board United Airlines Flight 175 came very quickly. First, the aircraft turned southwest without clearance. Then, at 8:46:48 a.m. EDT, seconds after American Airlines Flight 11 hit the North Tower, someone in the cockpit of United Flight 175 made the first of two rapid changes to its assigned transponder code. The flight also left its assigned altitude. Under normal circumstances, New York Center's Dave Bottiglia would have quickly noticed these developments, but he was involved in the ongoing search for the possibly hijacked American Flight 11. This task preoccupied him, particularly when he lost the radar feed on the American plane's primary track at 8:46:31. Bottiglia remained focused on American Flight 11, as reports came in about a fire at the World Trade Center, and, thereafter, as he continued to hunt for the plane, which he thought was heading south at a low altitude. About five minutes later, he noticed the changes to the United flight's transponder and repeatedly tried to contact the cockpit crew. At 8:53 a.m., just after the Otis F–15s were airborne and as radio reports began coming in about the crash of a commuter plane at the World Trade Center, Bottiglia warned another controller that he could not find United Flight 175 and that he feared it had been hijacked. This news, and the notion that military assistance was needed in the escalating situation, began to filter up over the next several minutes through the various levels of senior managers at New York Center, who then tried to contact regional managers.[188] They, however, "were discussing a hijacked aircraft (presumably American Flight 11) and refused to be disturbed."[189]

Ten minutes would pass before a New York Center staffer informed the NEADS air defenders of a "second possible hijack."[190] Just seconds later, they learned that a second plane, quickly identified as United Airlines Flight 175, had slammed into the South Tower at 9:03:11 EDT.[191] Nasypany, on the phone with Marr, told the battle commander that NEADS personnel had received an unconfirmed report of a "second hit from another aircraft." Marr, in the battle cab, and several other NEADS personnel had just seen the crash, live on CNN. The Otis fighters were at that moment south of Long Island,[192] and NEADS personnel were making an early effort to locate refueling tankers for them.[193]

The north and south towers of the World Trade Center were burning. Concerned that more aircraft out of Boston Logan Airport or elsewhere might still be "out there," hijacked and heading toward New York City, Nasypany wanted to move the Otis fighters out of military airspace in Whiskey 105 and place them, in coordination with FAA controllers, over Manhattan.[194]

Seeking "to establish a greater presence over New York," Nasypany also told the battle cab that he wanted to scramble the two armed alert F–16s at the 119th Fighter Wing, Detachment One, at Langley Air Force Base in southern Virginia and send them to the same location as the Otis fighters. But the battle cab declined his request and directed the NEADS mission crew commander to order the Langley fighters only to battle stations.[195]

On the morning of September 11, 2001, Marr had at his disposal only four armed fighters sitting strip alert with which to defend about a quarter of the country. Two of these, the Otis F–15s, were already airborne and holding in Whiskey 105; the other two were the Langley F–16s. Concerned about the Panta flight's fuel situation, Marr held the Langley fighters at battle stations, seeking to avoid having all of his fighters "in the air at the same time, which . . . [would mean that] they'd all run out of gas at the same time."[196] Marr and Arnold later recalled that the Langley fighters were put on battle stations rather than scrambled because they might be sent to relieve the Otis fighters if NEADS personnel could not find a refueling tanker quickly and also because of uncertainty about the developing situation in New York City.[197] Nasypany, too, recalled that the order to battle stations "was generated by the events taking place in New York." He noted that "the strategy was to 'lean forward'" in the event of another attack. His order sent the Langley fighters to battle stations "without a specific target," but he intended to use them "in response to another threat."[198]

In the meantime, no additional hijackings had been reported to NEADS. Nasypany's priorities were to move the Otis fighters closer to New York City, specifically south of Kennedy Airport, and to find and position refueling tankers to support them.[199] But the air defenders were merely "in the eye of the storm."[200] Unbeknownst to Arnold, Marr, Nasypany, or any of their subordinates, there had already been another hijacking, the third of the morning. In the time period between the two crashes at the World Trade Center, the Indianapolis Air Route Traffic Control Center had lost contact with a third aircraft, American Airlines Flight 77. Controllers there, unaware of the attacks in New York City,[201] initially believed that the plane had crashed due to electrical or mechanical trouble. Ironically, as NEADS and CONR leaders were considering ordering the Langley fighters to battle stations or to scramble, Indianapolis Center controllers were asking the Air Force Rescue Coordination Center at Langley Air Force Base to search for the possibly downed American flight.[202] United Airlines Flight 93, the fourth and final hijack, had at that point been in the air for more than twenty-five minutes and would be flying normally for another twenty.[203]

With FAA air traffic controllers working to clear airspace, NEADS directed the Panta flight to leave the holding pattern. The Otis F–15s arrived over New York City and established a combat air patrol over the city thirty-two minutes after becoming airborne.[204] The Otis fighters were the first on the scene of the disaster and represented the initial element of the U.S. military response to the terrorist attacks, but their defensive measure was too late to counter even the second attack. By the time they arrived, United Airlines Flight 175 was no more, and the south tower of the World Trade Center had been ablaze for almost twenty-two minutes.[205]

Duffy and Nash flew combat patrols over New York for the next several hours. Duffy set up a point defense, splitting the airspace to cover it in its entirety, and the two Otis pilots took turns refueling and intercepting.[206] During their time aloft, Duffy and Nash received requests from New York TRACON to identify a few civilian airliners and then, mostly, police and emergency response helicopters in coordination with NEADS.[207] Duffy later estimated that he and Nash intercepted "fifty or more" targets of interest, including general aviation aircraft, news helicopters, and even a number of Army Guard helicopters.[208]

The lull after the two attacks at the World Trade Center did not last long. The fog of war had begun to settle in almost immediately after the first strike, and confusion over what type of aircraft had hit the North Tower and questions about the status of American Airlines Flight 11 persisted. Then, in the minutes before Duffy and Nash established the combat air patrol over New York City, Boston Center passed to NEADS air defenders startling news from FAA headquarters: American Airlines Flight 11 was still airborne and was heading south toward Washington, D.C. Suddenly, NEADS personnel were faced with what was apparently a third hijacking, as whatever plane had hit the North Tower was thought, by many, *not* to have been Flight 11.[209]

After passing the Boston Center report to the battle cab, NEADS mission crew commander Nasypany advised the battle commander and the fighter officer there that NEADS needed to scramble the Langley fighters immediately.[210] In Nasypany's view, the Langley scramble should be placed over Baltimore, Maryland, to serve as "a 'barrier cap' between the hijack [American Airlines Flight 11, thought to be still aloft] and Washington, D.C."[211] Nasypany also told the battle cab that he wanted to direct the Otis fighters to "try to chase this guy [American Airlines Flight 11] down" if the aircraft could be found.[212]

But battle cab personnel were unenthusiastic about the latter recommendation.[213] Marr, the battle commander, later recalled that "he 'nixed' the tail chase—the Panta (Otis ANGB) fighters 'chasing down' A[merican] A[irlines Flight] 11, as reported heading south to Washington, D.C.—'as soon as' he heard of it."[214] Nasypany was, nevertheless, still concerned about the placement of the Panta flight. He told his weapons team that he wanted the Otis fighters closer to New York and was pleased to learn that they were already over it.[215] Nasypany's views on use of the Langley fighters were accepted by the battle cab, and Arnold and Marr approved scrambling the two fully armed Langley fighters on alert and a third F–16 armed with guns.[216]

On duty on the morning of September 11, 2001, at the Air National Guard detachment at Langley Air Force Base, were the senior and junior alert pilots, Maj. Dean F. Eckmann, a traditional Guardsman and commercial airline pilot, and Maj. Bradley M. "Lou" Derrig, a full-time Guardsman. On their schedule was a local training mission with Langley fighters from the First Fighter Wing, scheduled for a noon takeoff. After they received Nasypany's battle stations order, they were joined—as the result of an unprecedented order given by an officer in the NEADS battle cab—by the supervisor of flying, Capt. Craig D. "Borgy" Borgstrom, a full-time Guardsman.[217] Nasypany ordered the Langley alert fighters scrambled and headed toward Washington, D.C., under the call signs Quit 25 and 26, with Borgstrom as the pilot of a third fighter, Quit 27. The three Langley F–16s were airborne at 9:30 a.m. EDT.[218] Borgstrom later recalled that the Quit flight had "no mission on takeoff."[219]

Nasypany's original scramble order called for the Langley fighters to proceed on a 010 heading, flight level 290.[220] However, standard scramble procedures called for a takeoff to the east, toward Warning Area 386,[221] to get air defense fighters to altitude quickly and to avoid highly congested local airport traffic. With these and other considerations in mind, and not knowing about any additional hijackings or problematic aircraft, Langley Tower personnel entered a flight plan that directed the Quit flight to a heading of 090 for 60, or due east for sixty miles, flight level 290.[222] Eckmann later estimated that the Quit flight traveled east for forty-five miles before FAA air traffic controllers got them headed north, but the route as captured by radar indicated that the distance was sixty-nine nautical miles.[223]

Within a few minutes of the Langley fighters' takeoff, NEADS weapons desk personnel noticed that the Quit flight was off course and was not traveling in accordance with the scramble order. They immediately directed a U.S. Navy air traffic controller at Giant Killer to tell the Langley pilots to contact the NEADS air defenders on an auxiliary frequency and to redirect the flight toward Baltimore Washington International Airport, to intercept the phantom, presumed southbound, American Airlines Flight 11.[224]

American Airlines Flight 77

During a telephone call about American Airlines Flight 11 from the FAA's Washington Center to the Northeast Air Defense Sector,[225] the center's operations manager happened to mention to the air defenders that American Airlines Flight 77 was missing. The manager did not describe it as a hijacking. Less than four minutes later, Flight 77 crashed into the Pentagon.[226]

American Airlines Flight 77, a Boeing 757-223,[227] was scheduled to depart Washington Dulles International Airport at 8:10 a.m. EDT on a nonstop flight to Los Angeles International Airport. It pushed back from the gate at 8:09 a.m. and lifted off at 8:20 a.m. On board were a pilot, first officer, four flight attendants, and fifty-eight passengers, including five al Qaeda terrorists.[228] The flight proceeded normally until 8:51 a.m., when the cockpit crew made its last routine radio communication with Indianapolis Air Traffic Control Center. The hijackers attacked shortly thereafter. By 8:54 a.m., the aircraft was making a slight turn to the south, away from its assigned course. Three minutes later, someone in the cockpit turned off the transponder, and that individual or another—understanding the plane's internal communication system better than had the hijackers of American Airlines Flight 11—announced to the passengers over the plane's intercom that the flight had been hijacked. Ground control did not hear that communication. John Thomas, the Indianapolis Center controller tracking American Flight 77, noticed that the aircraft had deviated from its flight path and that the data tag disappeared. He could not find a primary radar return. Thomas, and soon thereafter, American Airlines dispatchers, tried repeatedly and unsuccessfully to contact the cockpit crew of American Flight 77 by radio. He and others at the center looked for the aircraft along its projected flight path and to the southwest, where it had started to alter course, but they did not look to the east. At that point, he did not know about the crashes at the World Trade Center or about any of the day's hijackings. He believed that American Flight 77 had gone down after suffering either a catastrophic mechanical or electrical failure, or both. Indianapolis Center contacted the Air Force Rescue Coordination Center at Langley Air Force Base at 9:08 a.m. and asked the service to search for a crashed airplane (*see* Table 5, American Airlines Flight 77 and 9/11 Commission Timeline, p 58).[229]

Meanwhile, the hijacker-pilot had further adjusted the aircraft's course, and the plane flew eastward, undetected for thirty-six minutes. Indianapolis Center personnel never saw the flight turn to the east. Initially, for more than eight minutes after the loss of its transponder, the flight's primary radar information was not displayed to Indianapolis Center controllers, in part because of poor radar coverage in its flight area. When American Flight 77 reappeared in primary radar coverage, a few minutes before Indianapolis Center contacted the Air Force Rescue and Coordination Center, Indianapolis Center controllers did not see it: they thought that the plane had crashed or was still heading west. By 9:20 a.m., Indianapolis Center staff had learned that other aircraft had been hijacked that morning, and they began thinking that American Flight 77 might have been as well. Information and concerns about the flight's status passed from the Indianapolis manager to the FAA Command Center at Herndon, to FAA field facilities, and even to FAA headquarters in Washington, D.C., but no one thought to ask for military assistance, and no one contacted NEADS. The Herndon command center did alert the terminal control facility at Dulles International Airport at 9:21 a.m. After several of its controllers found, at 9:32 a.m., an unidentified primary radar target traveling fast and east, Dulles notified Reagan National Airport, and FAA staff at both airports alerted a federal law enforcement agency charged with protecting the president.[230]

Around 9:34 a.m., as NEADS air defenders told a Navy air traffic controller at Giant Killer to redirect the Langley pilots toward Baltimore to intercept what was thought to be a southbound American Airlines Flight 11, NEADS identification desk personnel learned in a telephone call from the operations manager at Washington Center that Indianapolis Center had lost contact with American Airlines Flight 77. This, in fact, had happened forty minutes earlier, but during that time, the FAA had not so informed NEADS. During the phone call, American Flight 77 was not described as a possible hijacking.[231]

Just over a minute later, Boston Center told NEADS personnel that an unidentified aircraft—later determined to be the missing and presumed crashed American Airlines Flight 77—was six miles southeast of the White House, flying low and moving away.[232] Given the speed at which airliners travel, this meant, as Nasypany later recalled, that a possible attack was seconds away from the White House.[233] This threat ratcheted up the efforts of the NEADS air defenders to expedite the change of course for the Langley fighters and to get them over the Washington, D.C., area and to the White House as quickly and as directly as possible.[234] Nasypany, working with his weapons and surveillance teams, took the unusual step of declaring AFIO, authorization for interceptor operations,[235] a rarely used process by which NEADS air defenders could take, from FAA controllers, "immediate control of the airspace to clear a flight path for the Langley fighters."[236]

Almost exactly sixty minutes elapsed from the time NEADS personnel first learned from FAA air traffic controllers of the possible hijacking of American Airlines Flight 11 until Nasypany declared AFIO. During that hour, the NEADS air defenders had been dealing with five possible or actual aviation emergencies. The first was American Airlines Flight 11, thought by some to have been the plane that hit the north tower of the World Trade Center but was reportedly still airborne.[237] The second was the crash of a still-unidentified, still-unconfirmed plane at the North Tower. The third was the hijacking and crash of United Airlines Flight 175 at the South Tower. The fourth was the lost—that is, missing—American Airlines Flight 77. The fifth was the unidentified, low-flying aircraft moving away from the White House. Unbeknownst to anyone in the country—perhaps even to the hijacking planners themselves, who may have intended additional hijackings—the actual attacks would be over in less than thirty minutes. However, reports of suspected hijackings were only just beginning.

Immediately after the NEADS air defenders learned of the presence of the unknown deviating aircraft over Washington, D.C., the tracker technician who had been assigned by Nasypany to monitor the airspace over the general capital area spotted on radar what NEADS personnel believed was the errant plane. He established a primary radar track on the aircraft, Bravo 032, and observed it losing altitude. The technician lost it when the track faded quickly.[238]

Nasypany directed the technician to get a Z-point, or coordinate, on the vanished aircraft and then asked where the Langley fighters were located.[239] The Quit flight was, in fact, in Warning Area 386 and heading north, approximately 150 miles away from Washington, D.C. Nasypany, the NEADS air defenders, and Langley pilots Eckmann, Derrig, and Borgstrom did not know that the unidentified aircraft—American Airlines Flight 77—had slammed into the west side of the Pentagon at 9:37:46 a.m. EDT.[240] Its demise was confirmed by the crew of an unarmed National Guard C–130H cargo aircraft, which had spotted the flight shortly before impact. That crew, en route to Minnesota, would also report on the crash of United Airlines Flight 93, less than thirty minutes later.[241]

Seeking to expedite the arrival of the Langley fighters to the capital to intercept the unidentified aircraft, believed to be still airborne, Nasypany told his subordinates on the operations floor: "We need to get those back up there—I don't care how many windows you break!"[242] The mission crew commander later explained that his words were meant as "a direction for the Langley fighters to achieve supersonic speed."[243]

Because of limited communications, a mix-up in passing coordinates, and other issues, NEADS personnel could not fully or immediately implement Nasypany's intention or his declaration of authorization for interceptor operations. Northeast Air Defense Sector weapons technicians controlling the Langley flight, for example, had initially to relay communications—including heading and squawk information—through another aircraft and were not speaking directly with flight lead Eckmann, Quit 25, until several minutes after Nasypany's AFIO declaration.[244]

The NEADS air defenders first learned about the attack on the Pentagon from CNN about twelve minutes after American Airlines Flight 77 plowed into the west side of the building.[245] Also at 9:49 a.m. EDT, NORAD commander General Eberhart "directed all air sovereignty aircraft to battle stations, fully armed."[246] NEADS personnel were unaware of this order, at least initially. Still working with his standard four air alert aircraft, Nasypany again wondered about the location of the Langley fighters and twice expressed direction to place the Otis flight "over NCA [National Capital Area] now[.]"[247] But according to radar data, the Langley fighters did not arrive over Washington, D.C., until about 10:00 a.m. EDT.[248] Just under five minutes later, Quit 25 confirmed, in response to a NEADS query, that there was "smoke coming from the Pentagon[.]"[249]

United Airlines Flight 93

NEADS operations center personnel were not aware that United Airlines Flight 93 had been hijacked until just over four minutes after it had slammed into an abandoned strip mine[250] in Pennsylvania. Word of United Airlines Flight 93's last known latitude and longitude came during a call from a military liaison attached to the Federal Aviation Administration who was himself unaware that the aircraft had crashed. Twelve minutes after the crash, during a call initiated by the Northeast Air Defense Sector, the FAA informed the air defenders that the flight had gone down at an unknown location northeast of Camp David.[251]

United Airlines Flight 93, a Boeing 757-222,[252] was scheduled to depart Newark Liberty International Airport at 8:00 a.m. EDT on a nonstop flight to San Francisco International Airport. It pushed back from the gate at 8:00 a.m. but did not lift off until 8:42 a.m. On board were a pilot, first officer, five flight attendants, and thirty-seven passengers, including four al Qaeda terrorists. The flight proceeded normally for forty-six minutes, and the last routine communication between the flight deck and John Werth, the air traffic controller at Cleveland Air Route Traffic Control Center responsible for the flight, came at 9:25 a.m. At that point, the cockpit and cabin crews knew nothing of the morning's three hijackings or of the explosions in New York City. At 9:28 a.m., while the aircraft was flying at 35,000 feet over eastern Ohio, the hijackers attacked the cockpit crew. A struggle ensued. Just two minutes earlier, United Flight 93 pilot Jason Dahl had sent an ACARS* message asking United dispatcher Ed Ballinger to confirm a warning that Ballinger had just sent to the flight deck crew: "Beware any cockpit intrusion—Two a/c [aircraft] hit World Trade Center" (*see* Table 6, United Airlines Flight 93 and 9/11 Commission Timeline, p 59).[253]

In less than a minute of Dahl's ACARS message to Ballinger, Werth at Cleveland Center received two radio transmissions of unknown origin. The first contained sounds of a physical struggle and declarations of "Mayday," and the

---

*ACARS (Aircraft Communications and Reporting System) permits e-mailing between the in-flight cockpit crew and ground personnel.

second, shouts of "Hey get out of here" and screaming.[254] The aircraft's altitude suddenly dropped seven hundred feet. Werth began to contact other planes on his frequency to determine the source of the transmissions and continued to try to contact United Flight 93. A third radio transmission came over the frequency at 9:32 a.m.: "Keep remaining sitting. We have a bomb on board."[255] Like Mohammed Atta, the hijacker-pilot of American Airlines Flight 11, Ziad Jarrah, at the controls of United Flight 93, attempted to communicate with the passengers over the plane's intercom but ended up speaking to air traffic controllers on the ground. Werth told his supervisor that he thought the plane had been hijacked. Within two minutes, the information traveled up the chain of command to the command center at Herndon and then to FAA headquarters.[256]

There the information remained. Cleveland Center personnel, still tracking the United flight, asked the Herndon command center about 9:36 a.m. if anyone had asked the military to send fighters to intercept it and even offered to contact a local military base. The command center refused the offer, saying that FAA senior leaders had to make the decision to request military assistance and that they were discussing the matter. Eventually, Cleveland Center personnel took matters into their own hands and contacted NEADS personnel, but by then, United Airlines Flight 93 had already crashed. Meanwhile, thirteen minutes after Cleveland Center's initial inquiry about military involvement, the command center suggested to headquarters that someone there should probably decide, within the next ten minutes, whether to ask the military to scramble aircraft. Discussions at headquarters were ongoing between the deputy director for air traffic services and Monte Belger, the acting deputy administrator.[257]

The hijackers, however, had turned off the transponder on board United Flight 93, but not until 9:41, two minutes after a fourth radio transmission from Jarrah. The hijacker-pilot had intended to tell the passengers to remain seated and that the hijackers were returning to the airport to lodge their "demands," but this time, too, he pushed the wrong button and ended up again speaking to John Werth at Cleveland Center. Werth located the plane's primary radar return and tracked it as it altered course to the east and then to the south.[258]

At the same time that the Quit flight reached the nation's capital, and unbeknownst to NEADS personnel and the Langley pilots, the fourth and last plane hijacked on the morning of September 11 was in its final minutes of flight. Passengers and surviving crew on board United Airlines Flight 93 had already begun an assault on the cockpit in an attempt to wrest control of the plane from the four hijackers who had taken it over a little more than thirty minutes earlier.[259] The plane crashed in a field near Shanksville, Pennsylvania, at 10:03:11 a.m. EDT.[260] The NEADS air defenders did not learn until over three minutes later, in a telephone call from Cleveland Center's military liaison, that Flight 93 had even been hijacked.[261]

They had, however, heard about another possible hijack. Minutes after receiving the report of an unidentified aircraft near the White House and hearing

Nasypany's AFIO declaration, NEADS identification technicians learned from the FAA military liaison at Boston Center of the possible hijacking of Delta Airlines Flight 1989, then flying south of Cleveland, Ohio.[262] Its intentions were unknown, and it fit the profile of known hijackings up to that point on September 11. Like American Airlines Flight 11 and United Airlines Flight 175, the Delta plane was a Boeing 767 and had departed Boston Logan International Airport minutes after the American and United flights, full of fuel for a transcontinental journey, to Los Angeles.[263] But the Delta flight, despite its similarities to the first two commandeered aircraft, was not a hijacking at all. Its transponder had not been turned off or altered, and so FAA and NEADS personnel found and tracked it easily; its cockpit crew maintained communications with FAA air traffic controllers; and its alterations in course were a result of controllers' instructions to avoid colliding with United Airlines Flight 93, the hijacking of which FAA staff were aware but of which military personnel were not.[264]

In accordance with NEADS antihijacking protocol checklists, NEADS personnel did two things with respect to Delta Airlines Flight 1989 that were not done in connection with any of the aircraft hijacked on September 11. First, they designated Delta Airlines Flight 1989 a "Special 15" classification to aid in its tracking. Second, they not only established a track on the Delta flight, Bravo 089, but they also "forward told" the flight's track to NORAD.[265] Under agreed-upon procedures of the FAA and the DOD, whenever a hijacking occurred within radar coverage of one of the NORAD air defense sectors, the sector would forward—or "forward tell"—reports on the position of the errant plane to the Cheyenne Mountain Operations Center.[266]

As Delta Airlines Flight 1989 continued south of Toledo and then over Detroit, heading toward Chicago—raising a concern about a possible attack on Sears Tower—Nasypany and his air defenders were contacting other Air National Guard bases in the Great Lakes region and beyond—beginning with Toledo, Syracuse, Duluth, and Selfridge—to inquire about scrambling fighters. With the two Otis fighters over New York City, and the three Langley fighters heading toward Washington, D.C., Nasypany and Marr had to look beyond this small complement to ask for assistance from units that were not part of the nation's air defense alert force. Personnel at NEADS mentioned first the 180th Fighter Wing, an Ohio Air National Guard unit based at Toledo Express Airport, as a possible source for additional aircraft, and the wing got two F–16s airborne at 10:17 a.m. EDT. Nasypany quickly obtained an offer from the 127th Wing, a Michigan Air National Guard unit at Selfridge Air National Guard Base, of two F–16s that were in the air on a training mission, on which they had already expended their ordnance.[267] Cleveland Center personnel then asked about which fighters were being sent to intercept Delta Airlines Flight 1989 and how long it would take. With fighters at Duluth unavailable, Nasypany called his counterpart at the Western Air Defense Sector, who agreed to bring two armed fighters up at Fargo.[268]

By 10:00 a.m., as a result of concerns over the status of Delta Airlines Flight 1989, two Selfridge fighters were already airborne, and Toledo and Fargo promised two more each. Also available to Nasypany would soon be two F–16s, with guns, from Springfield, Ohio, that were returning from deployment at the Alpena Combat Readiness Training Center, as well as fighters from the Atlantic City Air National Guard.[269] Before ten minutes had passed, Nasypany's direct contact with the Western Air Defense Sector resulted in an offer of two additional fighters at Sioux City, Iowa.[270]

Meanwhile, Delta Airlines Flight 1989's transponder continued to function properly, and NEADS and FAA personnel continued to follow its flight path. It was, thus, the first questionable flight of the morning that might actually have been intercepted by aerial forces, at least two of which had weapons on board, before something untoward happened. It remained unclear, however, what if anything the pilots of those fighters should or could do if the flight proved to be hijacked or showed hostile intent. Seeking guidance from the battle cab on rules of engagement, Nasypany asked, "That special track over the . . . lake right now [Delta Flight 1989], so what are you gonna do with it, if it is [hijacked]. . . [?] What are we gonna do, I['ve] got to give my guys direction[.]"[271] The question remained unresolved during the entire attack period and for some time beyond.

At the same time that Nasypany and the battle cab were discussing what orders to pass to fighter pilots being scrambled against the Delta flight, the NEADS identification section was learning from Cleveland Center that the flight was in fact not hijacked. An identification team member had called the center to tell controllers there that two fighters each from Selfridge and Toledo had been scrambled in response to the Delta flight. She was surprised to learn from a center staffer that the Delta pilot was not being hijacked and was landing at Cleveland Airport "as a precaution because he took off from [Boston Logan.]"[272]

The simultaneous nature and speed of the 9/11 attacks made it increasingly difficult for the NEADS air defenders to keep an accurate count of the number of suspected hijackings. Misinformation about American Airlines Flight 11's being still airborne and about the possible hijacking of Delta Airlines Flight 1989 contributed to the fog of war. The pace of events slowed very briefly after the news from Cleveland Center that Flight 1989 was going to land without incident. But NEADS staff had at most only a few minutes' respite before they received a report from a NORAD unit in Canada that a Canadian commercial airliner, possibly hijacked and possibly out of Montreal, might be headed south toward Washington, D.C.[273] In the NEADS battle cab, Marr initially wanted New York Air National Guard fighters at Hancock Field, Syracuse, New York, to be sent against the Canadian flight.[274]

These plans changed quickly, however, when, within seconds, the NEADS air defenders faced a confirmed threat against a commercial aircraft much closer to home. Immediately after speaking with a Canadian NORAD staffer about the Canadian flight, a NEADS identification technician received from the military liaison at Cleveland Center a confirmed report of a bomb on board a non-transponding aircraft, United Airlines Flight 93. The military liaison asked about the possibility of redirecting to the last known location of the United flight the fighters from Selfridge and Toledo that had been scrambled against Delta Airlines Flight 1989. The terrible irony of this request was that, unbeknownst to Cleveland Center, United Airlines Flight 93 had crashed near Shanksville, Pennsylvania, over three minutes earlier, at 10:03:11 a.m. EDT.[275]

Shortly thereafter, Nasypany received a commitment from the Syracuse Air National Guard unit to launch four fighters, with hot guns, to search for United Airlines Flight 93 and Delta Airlines Flight 1989.[276] However, a NEADS identification technician then learned from the FAA's Washington Center that United Airlines Flight 93 had crashed.[277] The Syracuse fighters deployed at 10:44 a.m. EDT, more than forty minutes after Flight 93 crashed and more than fifteen minutes after the North Tower collapsed.[278]

The Immediate Post-Attack Period

The attacks of September 11, 2001, ended with the downing of United Airlines Flight 93, but no one knew that at the time. Nasypany, among others, had been concerned, after the strikes in New York City, that additional planes departing Boston might be hijacked,[279] and, later in the morning, that further attacks might be launched, in a cascading fashion, across the western time zones and perhaps overseas. Reports of additional possible hijackings and other suspicious incidents did continue for hours and even days thereafter.[280]

Just after Duffy and Nash were scrambled, six additional unarmed Otis F–15s had taken off on a training run to Warning Area 105. As they were flying over Martha's Vineyard, Lieutenant Colonel Treacy ordered them to return to Otis immediately.[281] By about 10:20 a.m., after Treacy had briefed the returning pilots about additional expected threats, a NEADS weapons controller called Otis Air National Guard Base on the scramble line and told personnel there to get all fighters in the air immediately. However, maintenance crews had discovered after the fighters returned from their training run that two of the six F–15s needed mechanical repairs before they could fly again. The four others—after all were refueled and at least some were armed—received orders to scramble and to establish combat air patrols over Boston. Thereafter, two of those fighters proceeded under orders to New York City "to work with, and then relieve" Duffy and Nash.[282]

District of Columbia Air National Guard F–16s of the 113th Wing, 121st Fighter Squadron, became involved in air defense operations over Washington, D.C., in the post-attack period. The 121st Fighter Squadron, based at Andrews Air Force Base, Maryland, was not an air defense alert unit.[283] Its personnel nevertheless responded when, about twenty minutes after American Airlines Flight 77 hit the Pentagon, the squadron received a White House request for a combat air patrol over the nation's capital.[284] The first of the Andrews fighters was airborne at 10:38 a.m. EDT, about thirty-five minutes after United Airlines Flight 93 crashed in Pennsylvania and ten minutes after the North Tower collapsed. The actual request for the Andrews F–16s had come from the federal law enforcement agency charged with protecting the president, not from within the military chain of command, and the fighters were dispatched without the foreknowledge of NEADS, NORAD headquarters, or military personnel at the NMCC at the Pentagon. Unbeknownst to those entities, most of the Andrews pilots scrambled on September 11 operated under instructions—given by that federal law enforcement agency to the 113th Wing commander, Brig. Gen. David F. Wherley, Jr.—that directed pilots "to protect the White House and take out any aircraft that threatened the Capitol." Wherley took this guidance to mean that the pilots were to fly "weapons free," that is, the shoot-down decision rested in the cockpit, specifically with the lead pilot, and he passed those orders to the pilots who took off at and after 10:42 a.m. EDT. These rules of engagement were quite different from those fighters launched under NORAD direction and are indicative of the chaos and turbulence engendered by the 9/11 attacks.[285]

Epilogue

The scope, complexity, and outcome of the 9/11 attacks were shocking and, seemingly, new and unprecedented. However, much about the terrorist operation—its connections with previous acts of Islamist terrorism, its perpetrators, their motivations, their tactics, and their targets—was not.

Of the nineteen hijackers, fifteen were Saudi nationals; two were United Arab Emirati nationals; one was a Lebanese national; and one, their leader, was an Egyptian national. The last, Mohammed Atta, was the operational head of al Qaeda's 9/11 "martyrdom operation" and the hijacker-pilot of American Airlines Flight 11, which crashed into World Trade Center 1, the north tower, in the first attack.[286] Behind the 9/11 hijackers stood a wider circle of instigators, planners, and accomplices, including Islamist regimes in Sudan and later in Afghanistan that gave al Qaeda safe harbor.

Even as the 9/11 attacks were unfolding, observers noted parallels to previous attacks planned by Osama bin Laden and executed by his al Qaeda network,[287] particularly the coordinated, nearly simultaneous bombings of two U.S. embassies in Kenya and Tanzania on August 7, 1998. Those attacks had come eight years to the day after Operation Desert Shield began and the first U.S. forces—F–15 fighters from Langley Air Force Base, Virginia—arrived in Saudi Arabia to protect the kingdom against a possible invasion by Saddam Hussein.[288] In the eyes of bin Laden and other Islamists, U.S. and other non-Muslim coalition forces were modern-day crusaders desecrating holy soil, and the United States was replacing the collapsing Soviet Union as an enemy of Islam and a threat to the region.[289]

Bin Laden's war against the United States had started earlier in the decade, when his rhetoric may have inspired, and al Qaeda support may have facilitated, several prominent jihadist attacks against U.S. persons and interests. These deadly operations included the December 1992 hotel bombings in Aden, Yemen; the February 1993 bombing, masterminded by Ramzi Yousef, of the World Trade Center;[290] the plot of May and June 1993, aided by Omar Ahmad Abdul Rahman, to destroy other landmarks in New York; the October 1993 killing of eighteen U.S. soldiers in the Battle of Mogadishu, Somalia; the December 1994 explosion on board a commercial jet flying from Manila to Tokyo, another of Yousef's plots, which killed one passenger; the November 1995 car bombing of the Saudi national guard facility in Riyadh, which killed five Americans; the June 1996 truck bombing of the U.S. sector of Khobar Towers housing complex in Dhahran, Saudi Arabia, which killed nineteen members of the U.S. Air Force's 4404th Wing (Provisional) and wounded five hundred more; and the November 1997 suicide attack and execution-style murders of fifty-eight foreign tourists and four Egyptians at Queen Hatshepsut's temple near Luxor, Egypt.[291]

By mid-summer 1996, al Qaeda was focusing less on supporting terrorist operations carried out by allied groups and more on executing actions supervised by bin Laden or his senior aides.[292] Bin Laden's fatwas, or religious rulings, of August 23, 1996[293] and February 23, 1998[294] declared war against the United States and his intention to launch attacks against U.S. military personnel, civilians, and allies anywhere in the world. Thereafter, the U.S. government became increasingly aware of bin Laden's involvement in, and al Qaeda's responsibility for, several deadly plots against the United States. These included the August 1998 East Africa embassy bombings, which injured 4,500 people and killed 224, including 12 Americans; attacks during the millennium period in the United States and elsewhere, including a bombing plot against Los Angeles International Airport that was thwarted with the December 1999 apprehension of Ahmed Ressam at Port Angeles, Washington; the January 2000 aborted suicide bombing against the U.S.S. *The Sullivans* in Aden; and the October 2000 suicide bombing of the U.S.S. *Cole,* also in Aden, which killed 17 U.S. sailors and injured 39 others.[295]

The 9/11 attacks were in some ways a traditional terrorist operation against a country that radical Islamists considered their religion's archenemy. Bin Laden intended them to devastate U.S. military power by destroying its foundation—the U.S. economy.[296] In an interview with the Arabic-language news network al-Jazeera in October 2001, bin Laden spoke proudly about the impact of the 9/11 attacks and the ruin of the World Trade Center towers:[297] "The values of this Western civilization under the leadership of America have been destroyed. Those awesome symbolic towers that speak of liberty, human rights, and humanity have been destroyed. They have gone up in smoke."[298]

Behind bin Laden's comments lay a view of history and the world that he shared with several generations of radical Islamists. In their moral universe, time is compressed. Military victories and defeats, humiliations and triumphs of centuries past, are part of their everyday outlook.[299] These notions were far removed from the experience of most Americans. In a speech on September 20, 2001, to a joint session of Congress and the nation, President George W. Bush spoke for many of his fellow citizens when he asked, "[W]hy do they hate us?"[300]

In the two decades before September 2001, the threat to U.S. citizens and interests had grown from a brand of terrorism inspired by a fundamentalist, extreme interpretation of Islam. Its adherents viewed God-given Islamic law, *sharia*, as the sole guide for the personal conduct of individuals and for the political behavior of governments. Islamists aimed, by violent means if necessary, to purify the Islamic world of what they considered the corruption, immorality, exploitative practices, and spiritual ignorance of non-Muslims and secular Muslims. Islamist fundamentalists generally sought to restore the caliphate and revive the religion's traditions and laws; overthrow secular, pro-Western regimes; destroy the Arab-Israeli peace process and the Jewish state; and expel Western nationals, including U.S. military personnel, from the Middle East.[301]

The forty-year period before the attacks of September 11, 2001, had seen increasingly deadly acts of violence carried out by international terrorist organizations against U.S. military personnel, diplomatic corps, aircraft, citizens, and interests overseas. In the 1970s and 1980s, such attacks were relatively infrequent and of limited effect.[302] Most terrorist groups were fairly small, and they and their state sponsors were motivated by ideology, politics, and domestic agendas.[303] In 1975, terrorism expert and RAND Corporation analyst Brian Jenkins wrote: "[T]errorists want a lot of people watching and a lot of people listening and not a lot of people dead." Two decades later, however, James Woolsey, Director of Central Intelligence, argued: "[T]oday's terrorists don't want a seat at the table; they want to destroy the table and everyone sitting at it."[304] The new terrorists were usually not just willing but eager to kill themselves as well.

In the intervening period, particularly after the Soviet Union's departure from Afghanistan in 1989, a new paradigm of terrorism had begun to emerge. In the 1990s, the number of terrorist attacks decreased, but casualties increased. The number of terrorist organizations motivated by religious concerns increased, and their members, disinterested in trying to win over their opponents, viewed violence against their enemies as a sacred act and a divine obligation. Against this background, mass, indiscriminate casualties became a goal.[305]

Exemplifying this new paradigm were the attacks planned or carried out against symbolic targets in the United States in the early 1990s by followers of Omar Abdul Rahman. The perpetrators, some of whom were U.S. citizens based largely in New Jersey, received religious sanction for their acts from Rahman, training or sanctuary in al Qaeda/bin Laden facilities, or financial support from bin Laden.[306] Their operations included the November 5, 1990, fatal shooting in Manhattan of Jewish extremist Meir Kahane by El-Sayyid Nosair;[307] the first World Trade Center bombing, on February 26, 1993, by Ramzi Yousef and other co-conspirators, that killed 6 people, injured 1,042 others, and caused $510 million in damage;[308] and the New York City landmarks multiple bomb plot, disrupted by the Federal Bureau of Investigation on June 23, 1993, for which Rahman and other defendants were later tried, convicted, and imprisoned in the United States.[309]

After the 1993 World Trade Center bombing, Yousef fled to the Philippines, where he was joined in the summer of 1994 by his uncle, Khalid Sheikh Mohammed. The two men developed Operation Bojinka, a scheme to blow up, over a two-day period over the Pacific Ocean, twelve passenger 747 aircraft of three major U.S. carriers. Investigations in the Philippines and in the United States later revealed that the plot also involved plans to assassinate President Bill Clinton, at the request of bin Laden; to murder Pope John Paul II; to bomb U.S.-bound cargo planes with explosive-laden jackets smuggled on board; and to crash an aircraft into the headquarters of the Central Intelligence Agency.[310]

The Bojinka plot, in its less well-known second wave, was later seen to strongly parallel the 9/11 attacks.[311] It involved Khalid Sheikh Mohammed's plan to crash aircraft into targets inside the United States, including, in New York, the World Trade Center; in the Washington, D.C. area, the Pentagon, the Capitol, and the White House; in San Francisco, the Transamerica Tower; in Chicago, the Sears Tower; and an unidentified nuclear plant.[312] The Bojinka scheme to send suicide operatives to train at U.S. flight schools, to commandeer commercial aircraft, and to fly them into high-profile U.S. targets became the sine qua non of the attacks of September 11, 2001.

In mid-1996, not long after bin Laden arrived in Afghanistan, Khalid Sheikh Mohammed briefed the al Qaeda chief and his military commander, Mohammed Atef (Abu Hafs al-Masri), on several attack plans that he and his nephew had developed in the summer of 1994 as part of the Bojinka plot. One called for suicide hijackers, trained as pilots, to fly airplanes into buildings in the United States. Bin Laden declined the proposals, but, apparently persuaded by Atef, he decided in late 1998 or early 1999 to support the hijacker-pilot plot. The three men met several times in Kandahar in the spring of 1999 to choose targets for what they were by then calling the "planes operation," and bin Laden began selecting suicide operatives.[313]

Suicide bombing attacks had sometimes been part of the old terrorism's arsenal, but they were becoming, increasingly, part of the new. Al Qaeda operatives commonly referred to suicide attacks as "martyrdom operations."[314] Those who volunteered for the missions believed that they were carrying out religiously justifiable—even obligatory—actions for their faith.[315] The notion of training suicide operatives to kill a passenger jet's flight crew, to take over the controls, and then to use the commandeered plane as a guided missile was in some ways an innovation. However, earlier terrorists had hijacked or attempted to hijack commercial aircraft intending to crash them into cities.[316]

The first attempt to use a commercial aircraft as a weapon occurred on September 5, 1986, by Palestinian suicide operatives hired by Libyan dictator Muammar Qaddafi to hijack Pan American Flight 73 and explode it over Tel

Aviv, Israel.[317] There were also cases in the United States of disturbed or disgruntled individuals such as Samuel Joseph Byck who, on February 22, 1974, tried to hijack Delta Airlines Flight 523 and force its pilot to crash the plane into the White House to assassinate President Richard M. Nixon.[318] Two decades later, in 1994, three other incidents received wide media coverage. The first, on April 7, involved Auburn Calloway, a Federal Express employee facing a disciplinary hearing, who assaulted the cockpit crew of FedEx Flight 705 in an attempt to gain control of the aircraft and crash it into a FedEx building in Memphis, Tennessee.[319] In the second, on the night of September 11/12, Frank Eugene Corder flew a stolen Cessna under radar in an attempt to crash the plane into the White House.[320] In the third, on December 24, four members of a subgroup of an Algerian terrorist organization, the Armed Islamic Group, stormed Air France Flight 8969, awaiting takeoff in Algiers.[321] After the hijackers killed three hostages, Algerian authorities allowed the flight to take off. The hijackers rigged the Airbus A300 with explosives and ordered it flown to Marseille and loaded with twenty-seven tons of fuel, about three times more than what would be required to fly to Paris, their proposed destination. On the ground at Marseille, the hijackers killed a fourth hostage on December 26. French antiterrorism commandos then stormed the plane, killing the hijackers and freeing the passengers. French investigators learned from the surviving hostages and from other sources that the hijackers had planned to blow up the aircraft over Paris or crash it into the Eiffel Tower.[322] Ramzi Yousef was alleged to have ties to the Armed Islamic Group, and Philippine investigators reportedly found a copy of *Time* magazine's cover story on the foiled attack among his possessions when they searched his Manila bomb-factory apartment in January 1995.[323]

Throughout the 1990s, it became more apparent that al Qaeda was a persistent and formidable adversary; that bin Laden had a longstanding intention to take his war to the United States; and that targets in New York City and the Washington, D.C., area were of particular interest.[324]

Al Qaeda's increasingly ambitious attacks against U.S. persons and interests were similar to those that Rahman called for at the beginning of the decade.[325] Officials in the Kahane murder investigation discovered a notebook of Nosair's, dated not later than 1990, that showed Rahman's possible inspiration for the World Trade Center attacks of 1993 and 2001. In it, a passage, probably copied from a speech by Rahman, called for "[t]he breaking and destruction of the enemies of Allah . . . by means of destroying exploding [sic], the structure of their civilized pillars such as the touristic infrastructure which they are proud of and their high world buildings which they are proud of and their statues which they endear [sic] and the buildings [in] which gather their head[s], their leaders. . . ."[326]

The evidentiary trail left after the first World Trade Center bombing in 1993[327] and a remark by Ramzi Yousef also suggested that al Qaeda intended to attack targets in New York City and to return most particularly to the World

Trade Center. Following his capture in Pakistan on February 7, 1995, Yousef was transferred that day to the United States on board a U.S. Air Force aircraft.[328] Authorities then flew him on an FBI helicopter to the Metropolitan Correctional Center in lower Manhattan. Along the way, an accompanying SWAT man had Yousef's blindfold removed and said, as they were flying alongside the World Trade Center, "You see, it's still standing." Yousef replied, "It wouldn't be if we had had more money."[329]

The destruction of the twin towers, for which Yousef had hoped and planned, was realized in the "planes operation" proposed by Khalid Sheikh Mohammed, supported by Mohammed Atef, and accepted by bin Laden. When the three men met in the spring of 1999 to select targets, Khalid Sheikh Mohammed suggested the World Trade Center, to complete the work his nephew had begun.[330] This time, the attackers would have more money. The appeal of the World Trade Center towers as targets for Islamist terror was constant and inalterable, from Rahman's call in 1990 to explode America's "civilized pillars" and "high world buildings" until Mohammed Atta and Marwan al-Shehhi crashed American Airlines Flight 11 and United Airlines Flight 175 into them on the morning of September 11, 2001.

Atef was killed in a U.S. air strike near Kabul, Afghanistan, in November 2001;[331] Khalid Sheikh Mohammed was captured in Rawalpindi, Pakistan, in March 2003 and was then held in U.S. custody at Guantánamo Bay, Cuba;[332] and bin Laden was killed in Abbottabad, Pakistan, by U.S. Special Forces in May 2011.[333] Al Qaeda's general command announced in mid-June 2011 that Ayman al-Zawahiri (b. 1951), bin Laden's longtime deputy, would take over as head of the network.[334] Despite these and other losses and almost ten years after the 9/11 hijackings, al Qaeda and allied groups remained keenly interested in attacking high-value U.S. targets, including commercial aviation. A dual U.S.-Yemeni citizen, Anwar al-Awlaki, and the Yemen-based organization, Al Qaeda in the Arabian Peninsula (AQAP),[335] were linked to the Christmas Day 2009 attempted bombing of Northwest Airlines Flight 235 over Detroit by Umar Farouk Abdulmutallab; to the October 2010 bomb plot against U.S. and other cargo and passenger planes; and to the May 2010 failed car bombing in New York City's Times Square by another U.S. citizen, Faisal Shahzad.[336] Al-Awlaki had also been linked to three of the hijackers of American Airlines Flight 77 and to Nidal Malik Hasan, later a U.S. Army major and psychiatrist accused of thirteen counts of premeditated murder in the November 2009 massacre at Fort Hood, Texas.[337]

A decade after the attacks of September 11, 2001, the "new type of war" that confronted NEADS air defenders that morning and the resulting new mission for U.S. Air Force pilots, the possible shoot-down of a U.S. passenger aircraft, were no longer new. Given the continuing and evolving terrorist threat against aviation, it was unlikely that either the war or the mission would end in the near future.

NORAD Air Defense Structure on 9/11

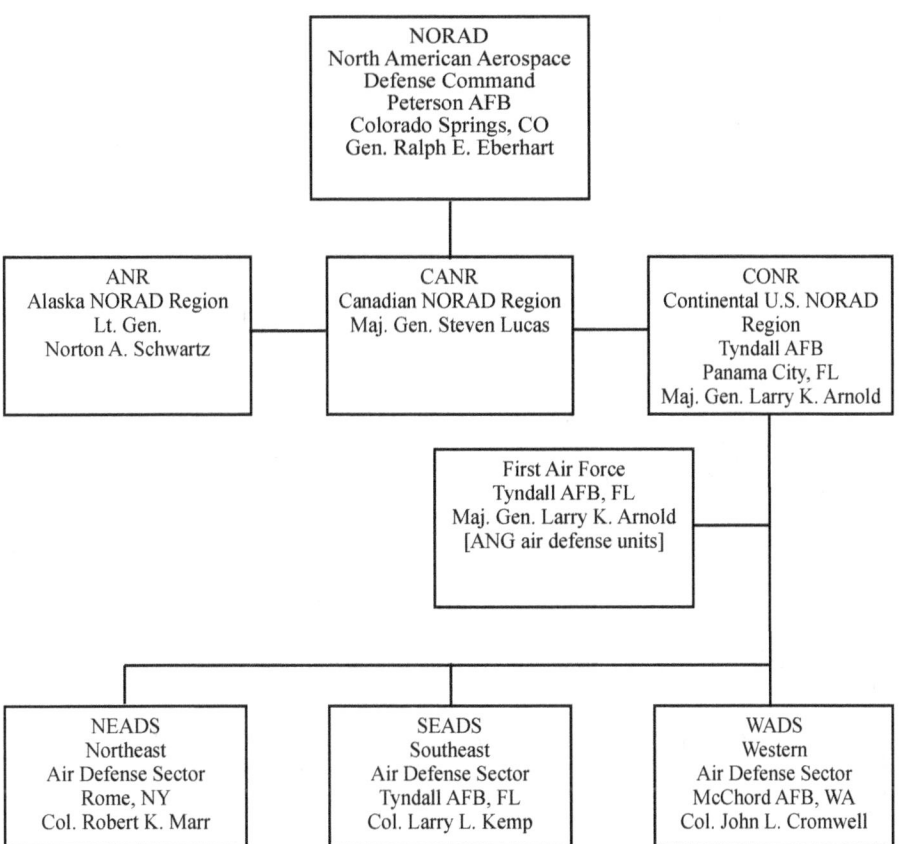

Source: Leslie Filson, *Air War Over America: Sept. 11 alters* [sic: the] *face of* [sic: the] *air defense mission* (Tyndall Air Force Base, Fla.: Headquarters 1st Air Force, Public Affairs Office, 2003), pp v, 5, 6, 24, 34, 42, 50, 52, and 71.

Table 1
Timing of FAA Notification to NORAD's Northeast Air Defense Sector
(all times are EDT)

Flight and Event	American Airlines Flight 11	United Airlines Flight 175	American Airlines Flight 77	United Airlines Flight 93
Last routine communication	Just before 0814	0842	0851	0927
First sign of trouble	0814 or shortly thereafter	0847	0854	0928:17
FAA believes flight in distress	0825	0853–0855	0856–0900	0934 (FAA ATC in charge of flight had concluded this at first sign of trouble)
FAA notifies NEADS	0837:52	0903	0934: FAA told NEADS AAL 77 missing	1007: FAA told NEADS UAL 93 hijacked
Fighter battle stations order (Otis ANGB)	0841:32 (2 F–15s: Otis ANGB, Falmouth, MA)			
Fighter scramble order (Otis ANGB)	0845:54	See AAL 11		
Fighters airborne (Otis ANGB)	0852	See AAL 11		
Airline impact time	0846:25: WTC 1 Collapsed: 1028:22	0903:11: WTC 2 Collapsed: 0958:59	0937:46: Pentagon	1003:11: PA
Elapsed time: FAA believes flight in distress until FAA notifies NEADS	12 minutes 52 seconds	8–10 minutes	34–38 minutes	33 minutes
Elapsed time: FAA notifies NEADS until crash	8 minutes 33 seconds	11 seconds	3 minutes 46 seconds	Minus 3 minutes 49 seconds
FAA notification to NEADS: AAL 11 still airborne	0921:10 (First mentioned about 0856:31)			
Fighter battle stations order (Langley AFB)	0909 (2 F–16s: Langley AFB, Hampton, VA)			
Fighter scramble order (Langley AFB)	0924 (Scramble order included a third F–16, with guns)			
Fighters airborne (Langley AFB)				

Source: *The 9/11 Commission Report: Final Report of the National Commission on Terrorist Attacks Upon the United States* (Washington, D.C.: Government Printing Office, 2004), Chapter 1, "We Have Some Planes" [http://www.9-11commission .gov/report/911Report_Ch1.pdf, accessed Aug 20, 2007].

Table 2
General Overview of the Four Hijacked Flights
(all times are EDT)

	American Airlines Flight 11	United Airlines Flight 175	American Airlines Flight 77	United Airlines Flight 93
Airplane make/model	Boeing 767-223	Boeing 767-222	Boeing 757-223	Boeing 757-222
Registration number	N334AA	N612UA	N644AA	N591UA
Itinerary	Boston Logan International Airport (BOS)-Los Angeles International Airport (LAX)	Boston Logan International Airport (BOS)-Los Angeles International Airport (LAX)	Washington Dulles International Airport (IAD)-Los Angeles International Airport (LAX)	Newark Liberty International Airport (EWR)-San Francisco International Airport (SFO)
Passengers and crew	Passengers: 81 (including 5 hijackers) Crew: 11 (9 cabin and 2 flight deck) Total: 92	Passengers: 56 (including 5 hijackers) Crew: 9 (7 cabin and 2 flight deck) Total: 65	Passengers: 58 (including 5 hijackers) Crew: 6 (4 cabin and 2 flight deck) Total: 64	Passengers: 37 (including 4 hijackers) Crew: 7 (5 cabin and 2 flight deck) Total: 44
Scheduled departure time	0745	0800	0810	0800
Push-back time	0740	0758	0809	0800
Wheels-off time	0759	0814	0820	0842
Impact time	0846:25	0903:11	0937:46	1003:11
Crash site	New York City WTC 1 (North Tower)	New York City WTC 2 (South Tower)	Arlington, VA Pentagon	Shanksville, PA Empty field

Source: *The 9/11 Commission Report: Final Report of the National Commission on Terrorist Attacks Upon the United States* (Washington, D.C.: Government Printing Office, 2004), [http://www.9-11commission.gov/report/911Report_Ch1.pdf, accessed Aug 20, 2007].

Table 3	
American Airlines Flight 11 and 9/11 Commission Timeline (all times are EDT)	
Event	**9/11 Commission Timeline**
Takeoff (wheels off)	0759
Last routine communication	Just before 0814
First sign of trouble	Just before 0814
Likely takeover	0814 or shortly thereafter
Transponder turned off	0821[338]
Initially unintelligible transmission of unknown origin heard by Boston Center air traffic control specialist	0824:38
Second suspect transmission heard by Boston Center air traffic control specialist	0824:57[339]
FAA believes flight in distress (hijacked)	0825
AAL 11 begins southbound turn over Albany, NY	0826[340]
Third suspect transmission heard by Boston Center air traffic control specialist and his section	0834[341]
FAA notifies NEADS	0837:52
Fighter scramble order: 2 F–15s from Otis ANGB, Falmouth, MA	0845:54
Fighters airborne, Otis ANGB	0852
Airline impact time: WTC 1	0846:25
Elapsed time: FAA believes flight in distress (hijacked) until FAA notifies NEADS	12 minutes 52 seconds
Elapsed time: FAA notification to NEADS until crash	8 minutes 33 seconds
FAA notification to NEADS: AAL 11 still airborne	0921:10
Fighter scramble order: 2 F–16s from Langley AFB, Hampton, VA. Scramble order included third aircraft	0924
Fighters airborne, Langley AFB	0930

Source: *The 9/11 Commission Report: Final Report of the National Commission on Terrorist Attacks Upon the United States* (Washington, D.C.: Government Printing Office, 2004), [http://www.9-11commission.gov/re port/911Report_Ch1.pdf, accessed Aug 20, 2007]; Miles Kara, e-mails to P. D. Jones, Jun 6, 2011, 5:36 p.m. and 10:19 p.m. EDT; and Jun 7, 2011, 1:20 p.m. EDT.

Table 4 United Airlines Flight 175 and 9/11 Commission Timeline (all times are EDT)	
Event	**9/11 Commission Timeline**
Takeoff (wheels off)	0814
Last routine communication	0842
First sign of trouble	0847
Transponder code changed	0847
FAA believes flight in distress	0853–0855
FAA notifies NEADS	0903
Fighter scramble order	See AAL 11
Fighter airborne: Otis ANGB	See AAL 11
Airline impact time: WTC 2	0903:11
Elapsed time: FAA believes flight in distress until FAA notifies NEADS	8–10 minutes
Elapsed time: FAA notification to NEADS until crash	11 seconds

Source: *The 9/11 Commission Report: Final Report of the National Commission on Terrorist Attacks Upon the United States* (Washington, D.C.: Government Printing Office, 2004), [http://www.9-11com mission.gov/re port/911Report_Ch1.pdf, accessed Aug 20, 2007].

Table 5
American Airlines Flight 77 and 9/11 Commission Timeline
(all times are EDT)

Event	9/11 Commission Timeline
Takeoff (wheels off)	0820
Last routine communication	0851
First sign of trouble	0854
Transponder turned off	0856
FAA believes flight in distress	0856–0900
FAA notifies NEADS	0934: FAA told NEADS AAL 77 missing
Fighter scramble order	
Fighters airborne	
Airline impact time: Pentagon	0937:46
Elapsed time: FAA believes flight in distress until FAA notifies NEADS	34–38 minutes
Elapsed time: FAA notification to NEADS until crash	3 minutes 46 seconds

Source: *The 9/11 Commission Report: Final Report of the National Commission on Terrorist Attacks Upon the United States* (Washington, D.C.: Government Printing Office, 2004), [http://www.9-11com mission.gov/re port/911Report_Ch1.pdf, accessed Aug 20, 2007].

Table 6
United Airlines Flight 93 and 9/11 Commission Timeline
(all times are EDT)

Event	9/11 Commission Timeline
Takeoff (wheels off)	0842
Last routine communication	0926–0927
First sign of trouble	0928:17
FAA believes flight in distress	0934
Transponder turned off	0941
FAA notifies NEADS	1007: FAA told NEADS UAL 93 hijacked
Fighter scramble order	
Fighters airborne	
Airline impact time: Shanksville, PA	1003:11
Elapsed time: FAA believes flight in distress until FAA notifies NEADS	33 minutes
Elapsed time: FAA notification to NEADS until crash	Minus 3 minutes 49 seconds

Source: *The 9/11 Commission Report: Final Report of the National Commission on Terrorist Attacks Upon the United States* (Washington, D.C.: Government Printing Office, 2004), [http://www.9-11com mission.gov/re port/911Report_Ch1.pdf, accessed Aug 20, 2007].

Notes

1. Government officials, academics, linguists, and journalists often spell Arabic names differently. Even the same government department, for example, may render Osama bin Laden's network as "al Qaeda" in one text and as "al-Qaeda" in another. Similarly, "Osama" may appear as "Usama" and "bin Laden" as "bin Ladin." In this publication, "al Qaeda" and "Osama bin Laden" are used.

2. Lawrence Wright, *The Looming Tower: Al-Qaeda and the Road to 9/11* (New York: Alfred A. Knopf, 2007), pp 72 and 393–94 (endnote for p 72 about the lack of definitive information on bin Laden's date of birth). The White House, President Barack H. Obama, Office of the Press Secretary, Remarks by the President on Osama Bin Laden, The White House, East Room, Washington, D.C., May 2, 2011, 11:35 p.m. EDT. [http://www.whitehouse.gov/the-press-office/2011/05/02/remarkspresident-osama-bin-laden, accessed May 2, 2011.]

3. Wright, *The Looming Tower*, pp 235–36, 307–308.

4. Dan Eggen and Vernon Loeb, "U.S. Intelligence Points To Bin Laden Network," *Washington Post*, Sep 12, 2001, p A1.

5. Early in the afternoon of Sep 11, 2001, Senator Chuck Hagel (R-Neb.) told reporters that the 9/11 attacks were "the second Pearl Harbor." Direct quote of Hagel in Jake Tapper, "Bush, Challenged," Salon.com, Sep 12, 2001. [http://www.salon.com/politics/feature/2001/09/11/bush/print.html, accessed Jun 12, 2008.]

6. Michael Grunwald, "Bush Promises Retribution; Military Put on Highest Alert," *Washington Post*, Sep 12, 2001, p A1.

7. Data on the security of the U.S. civil aviation system from *Staff Monograph on the Four Flights and Civil Aviation Security*, 9/11 Commission Staff Report dated Aug 26, 2004, 2d version, released by the U.S. Department of Justice on Sep 12, 2005, Part II: "Civil Aviation Security and the 9/11 Attacks" (hereinafter *Staff Monograph*, Part II), p 53f., and p 102, endnote 426. [http://www.archives.gov/ legislative/research/9-11/staff-report-sept2005.pdf, accessed Mar 3, 2008.] (The second version contains less redacted information than the first version, which was released on Jan 28, 2005.) Additional general information from Michael Bronner, "9/11 Live: The NORAD Tapes," *Vanity Fair*, Aug 2006 [http://www.vanityfair.com/ politics/features/2006/08/norad200608, accessed May 1, 2008]; Scot J. Paltrow, "Government Accounts of 9/11 Reveal Gaps, Inconsistencies," *Wall Street Journal Online*, Mar 22, 2004 [http://online.wsj.com/ article_print/0,,SB107991342102561383,00.html, accessed Mar 21, 2004]; "September 11: Chronology of Terror," CNN.com, Sep 12, 2001, posted 12:27 p.m. EDT [http://archives.cnn.com/2001/US/09/ 11/chronology.attack/index.html, accessed Sep 5, 2007]; Andrea Stone, "Pentagon's 'Primary Mission' Now Homeland Defense," *USA Today*, Sep 30, 2001, updated 10:07 p.m. E[D]T [http://www.usa today.com/news/sept11/2001/09/30/pentagon-review.htm, accessed Jul 9, 2008]; and *Quadrennial Defense Review Report*, Department of Defense, Sep 30, 2001 [http://www.comw.org/qdr/qdr2001.pdf, accessed Jul 9, 2008]; Dana Milbank, "White House Staff Switches Gears," *Washington Post*, Sep 17, 2001, p 25. General information from *The 9/11 Commission Report: Final Report of the National Commission on Terrorist Attacks Upon the United States* (hereinafter *The 9/11 Commission Final Report*) (Washington, D.C.: Government Printing Office, 2004), pp 4, 14, 32, and 33 and p 452, endnote 24, citing NTSB [National Transportation and Safety Board] report, "Air Traffic Control Recording—American Airlines Flight 11," Dec 21, 2001; p 457, endnote 89, citing Flight 93 FDR [flight data recorder] and CVR [cockpit voice recorder] data; full details on p 456, endnote 70, NTSB report, "Specialist's Factual Report of Investigation—Digital Flight Data Recorder" for United Airlines Flight 93, Feb 15, 2002; FBI report, "CVR from UA Flight #93," Dec 4, 2003 [http://www.9-11commission.gov/report/911Report_Ch1.pdf, accessed Aug 20, 2007.]

8. *The 9/11 Commission Final Report*, p 46 (direct quotation of Bianchi) and p 466, endnote 241, citing NEADS audio file, Identification Technician [ID Tech] position, recorder 1, channel 4, 10:02:22 [a.m. EDT]. In another source, Bianchi's words are rendered as "A new type of war, that's what it is." Direct quote from "9/11 NEADS Tape Transcription, DRM 1, DAT 2, Channel 4, ID Op," transcribed by Janet S. Dickens from the audiotapes provided [by the 9/11 Commission] to Alderson Reporting, p 39. N.d. [http://www.scribd.com/doc/14142075/NYC-Box-3-Neadsconrnorad-Fdr-Transcript-Neads-Channel-4-Id-Op, accessed Dec 11, 2009. Steve Bianchi was working at NEADS as a mission crew commander technician (MCC Tech) on Sep 11, 2001. National Commission on Terrorist Attacks Upon

the United States (hereinafter 9/11 Commission), "Memorandum for the Record (hereinafter MFR) of the Interview of Steve Bianchi of the NEADS Conducted by Team 8, 10/27/2003," Record Group (RG) 148: Records of Commissions of the Legislative Branch, 1928–2006, Center for Legislative Archives, U.S. National Archives & Records Administration (hereinafter NARA), Washington, D.C. [http://media.nara.gov/9-11/MFR/t-0148-911MFR-00769.pdf, accessed Jan 27, 2009.]

9. White House, transcript, "The Vice President appears on Meet the Press with Tim Russert," Camp David, Md., Sep 16, 2001. [http://www.whitehouse.gov/vicepresident/news-speeches/speeches/vp20010916.html, accessed Aug 27, 2008.]

10. Lynn Spencer, author of *Touching History: The Untold Story of the Drama That Unfolded in the Skies over America on 9/11* (New York/London/Toronto/Sydney: Free Press, 2008) pointed out the importance of analyzing who, specifically, at NEADS was notified, when, and by whom at FAA, again, specifically. Oral history interview of Lynn Spencer, conducted by Dr. Priscilla D. Jones on Apr 3, 2009, at the Air Force Historical Studies Office (AFHOH), Bolling AFB, D.C.

11. Leslie Filson, *Air War Over America: Sept. 11 alters* [sic: the] *face of* [sic: the] *air defense mission* (Tyndall Air Force Base, Fla.: Headquarters 1st Air Force, Public Affairs Office, 2003), pp v, 5, 6, 24, 34, 42, 50, 52, and 71; Ted Jackovics, "Post-9/11 air defense gaps leave cities on fringes of response time," Tampa Tribune, TBO.com, Tampa Bay Online, Apr 19, 2010. [http://www2.tbo.com/content/2010/apr/19/post-911-air-defense-has-gaps/news-politics/, accessed Apr 12, 2011.]

12. 9/11 Commission, "[MFR] of a Visit to 119th Fighter Wing of the U.S. Air Force Conducted by Team 8, 10/07/2003," RG 148: Records of Commissions of the Legislative Branch, 1928–2007, Center for Legislative Archives, U.S. National Archives & Records Administration [NARA], Washington, D.C. [http://media.nara.gov/9-11/MFR/t-0148-911MFR-00677.pdf, accessed Oct 27, 2009]; 9/11 Commission, "[MFR] of an Interview with Donald J. Quenneville of the United States Air Force Conducted by Team 8, 01/07/2004," RG 148: Records of Commissions of the Legislative Branch, 1928–2007, Center for Legislative Archives, NARA, Washington, D.C. [http://media. nara.gov/9-11/MFR/t-0148-911MFR-00916.pdf, accessed Oct 27, 2009]; *The 9/11 Commission Report*, p 17.

13. U.S. General Accounting Office, National Security and International Affairs Division, Report to Congressional Committees, *Continental Air Defense: A Dedicated Force Is No Longer Needed*, GAO/NSIAD-94-76, May 3, 1994, Richard Davis, Director, National Security Analysis, pp 4, 9, 14–16, quotes on p 15.

14. Ibid., p 2.

15. Ibid., p 1.

16. Ibid., pp 1 and 2, quote on p 2.

17. On Nov 27, 2002, President George W. Bush signed Public Law 107-306, the legislation establishing the National Commission on Terrorist Attacks Upon the United States, more commonly known as the 9/11 Commission. The commission closed on Aug 21, 2004. Thomas H. Kean and Lee H. Hamilton, with Benjamin Rhodes, *Without Precedent: The Inside Story of the 9/11 Commission* (New York: Alfred A. Knopf, 2006), pp 34–40, 350; and 9/11 Commission website frozen on Sep 20, 2004, at 12:00 a.m. EDT, and now a federal record managed by the National Archives and Records Administration [http://govinfo.library.unt.edu/911/archive/index.htm, accessed Dec 20, 2007]. With respect to the end date of the 9/11 Commission, cf., U.S. Department of Transportation, Office of the Secretary of Transportation, Office of Inspector General [OIG], "Results of OIG Investigation of 9/11 Commission Staff Referral," Aug 31, 2006, Project ID: CC-2006-085, attaching a memorandum from Todd J. Zinser, Acting Inspector General, to the [unnamed] Acting Secretary, Federal Aviation Administrator, Aug 31, 2006, subj: ACTION: Results of OIG Investigation of 9/11 Commission Staff Referral. The Zinser memorandum cites 9/11 Commission general counsel Daniel Marcus's referral letter to the DOD and DOT Inspectors General, Jul 29, 2004, as stating that the commission would "sunset" on Aug 26, 2004. [http://www.oig.dot.gov/item.jsp?id=1881, accessed Nov 19, 2007.]

18. *The 9/11 Commission Final Report*, "Notes," p 449; Kean and Hamilton, *Without Precedent*, p 257.

19. Philip Shenon, *The Commission: The Uncensored History of the 9/11 Investigation* (New York and Boston: Twelve, 2008), p 118. Department of Defense, Inspector General, memorandum from Shelton R. Young, Deputy Inspector General for Intelligence, to the [unnamed] Under Secretary of Defense for Intelligence, Sep 12, 2006, subj: Report on Review of Testimony to the National Commission on Terrorist Attacks Upon the United States (Report No. 06-INTEL-12), and referring to a March 2004 letter written to the 9/11 Commission by the commanding general of the North American Aerospace

Defense Command (NORAD). The unnamed general, who was in fact Gen Ralph E. Eberhart, acknowledged that the 9/11 Commission's revised timeline was accurate.

20. *The 9/11 Commission Final Report*, pp 20 and 21, and p 458, particularly endnotes 115 and 116; Bronner, "9/11 Live: The NORAD Tapes," Aug 2006.

21. Bronner, "9/11 Live: The NORAD Tapes," Aug 2006, quote from ID Tech SrA Stacia Rountree at 9:03:17 a.m. [EDT]. Rountree fielded the phone call from the FAA's New York Center on Long Island. *The 9/11 Commission Final Report*, p 23 and p 460, endnote 134, relied here on FAA and NEADS interviews, rather than on the NEADS operations floor audio files, which are the source for Bronner's article.

22. *The 9/11 Commission Final Report*, p 26 and p 461, endnote 148, citing NEADS audio file, ID Tech position, channel 7, 9:21:10 a.m.

23. Bronner, "9/11 Live: The NORAD Tapes," Aug 2006, NEADS audio tape, 8:56:31 a.m. [EDT].

24. Bronner, "9/11 Live: The NORAD Tapes," Aug 2006; *The 9/11 Commission Final Report*, p 27 and p 461, endnotes 151 and 154, citing NEADS audio files and interviews; and 9/11 Commission analysis of FDR [flight data recorder], air traffic control, radar, and Pentagon elevation and impact site data.

25. "Scene of utter destruction," *Pittsburgh Tribune-Review*, Sep 12, 2001. [http://www.pittsburghlive.com/x/pittsburghtrib/s_12940.html, accessed Sep 24, 2008]; *The 9/11 Commission Final Report*, pp 30 and 31, and p 462, endnotes 171, 173, and 174, citing NEADS audio files and log book.

26. 9/11 Commission, MFR, 119th Fighter Wing, 10/07/2003, RG 148, NARA, Washington, D.C.

27. Early media reports and government agency news releases on the air defense response launched on the morning of September 11, 2001, were often incomplete or inaccurate. Despite their often problematic nature, these preliminary reports and releases, together with the faulty timelines presented by the FAA and NORAD in the days following the attacks and in public testimony months and years later, had a substantial effect on public opinion. By the time the 9/11 Commission began its investigations in early 2003, public views of the air defense response had hardened significantly. Factual errors in early news reports, government statements, and public testimony on the matter were not easily corrected, and resulting misperceptions on the part of the public were not easily revised. However, as years passed, the print and internet publication of and extensive media commentary on the commission's staff reports, public hearings, and *The 9/11 Commission Final Report* provided a more accurate understanding of the attacks and of the air defense response they provoked. Notable in this regard also were the Office of Inspector General reports of the Departments of Transportation and Defense, which were published in complete or redacted versions beginning in August 2006.

28. *The 9/11 Commission Final Report*, p 20 and pp 458–59, endnotes 115–120, citing, e.g., 9/11 Commission interviews of CONR, NEADS, Otis ANGB, and FAA personnel; and NEADS audiotapes; Bronner, "9/11 Live: The NORAD Tapes," Aug 2006, NEADS audio tape, 8:37:52 a.m. [EDT].

29. Ibid., pp 26–27 and p 461, endnotes 148–150, citing NEADS interview and audio files: ID Tech position, channel 7, 9:21:10 a.m. EDT; MCC, channel 2, 9:21:50 and 9:22:34 a.m. EDT.

30. John Raidt, "Memo for Record," re: FAA Ops [Operations] Center [a.k.a. Washington Operations Complex (WOC), FAA Headquarters] Visit, date of visit: Jun 4, 2003. [http://www.scribd.com/doc/17053249/T8-B1-FAA-Command-Center-Briefing-6403-Fdr-3-MFRs-and-2-Withdrawal-Notices-710, accessed Nov 3, 2009.]

31. *The 9/11 Commission Final Report*, p 45.

32. Robert D. McFadden, "U.S. Details Careful Plan Of Hijacker," *New York Times*, Feb 13, 1993, section 1, p 23. [http://www.nytimes.com/1993/02/13/nyregion/us-details-careful-plan-of-hijacker.html, accessed Mar 24, 2009.] The hijacking of Lufthansa Airlines Flight 592 was the first trans-Atlantic act of air piracy since Sep 1976. 9/11 Commission undated, unsigned miscellaneous working papers re flights, response tables, timelines: information on Lufthansa Airlines Flight 592 and table comparing Lufthansa Airlines Flight 592 and American Airlines Flight 11. [http://www.scribd.com/doc/13723810/T8-B16-Misc-Work-Papers-Fdr-4-Stapled-Pgs-Re-Flights-Response-Tables-Time-Lines-Summary-134, accessed May 27, 2009]; *Criminal Acts Against Civil Aviation 1993*, annual report (Washington, D.C.: Federal Aviation Administration, Office of Civil Aviation Security), p 28.

33. 9/11 Commission, "[MFR] of the Interview of Robert Marr of the NEADS Conducted by Team 8, 01/23/2004," RG 148: Records of Commissions of the Legislative Branch, 1928–2006, Cen-

ter for Legislative Archives, NARA, Washington, D.C. [http://media.nara.gov/9-11/MFR/t-0148-911MFR-00767.pdf, accessed Jan 21, 2009]; Spencer, *Touching History*, pp 26–27.

34. 9/11 Commission, "[MFR] of the NEADS Briefing with Shelley Watson, Stacie Roundtree [sic: Stacia Rountree], [Maureen] Dooley, Fred Davies of NEADS Conducted by Team 8, 10/27/2003," [This MFR actually covers Robert Marr's initial briefing to 9/11 Commission staff.] RG 148: Records of Commissions of the Legislative Branch, 1928–2007, Center for Legislative Archives, NARA, Washington, D.C. [http://media.nara.gov/9-11/MFR/t-0148-911MFR-00762.pdf, accessed Jan 21, 2009.]

35. Duffy later told 9/11 Commission staff that another lieutenant colonel, Ramsey [first name not indicated], was the lead on the Lufthansa scramble. 9/11 Commission, "[MFR] of an Interview with Timothy Duffy of the United States Air Force Conducted by Team 8, 01/07/2004," RG 148: Records of Commissions of the Legislative Branch, 1928–2006, Center for Legislative Archives, NARA, Washington, D.C. [http://media.nara.gov/9-11/MFR/t-0148-911MFR-00915.pdf, accessed Jun 18, 2009]; Oral history interview with Col. Tim Duffy conducted at Tyndall AFB, Fla., Aug 12, 2009, by Troy Johnson and Bruce Stewart, First Air Force History Office (1 AF/HO), and Dr. Mary Dixie Dysart, AFHRA/RS; Spencer, *Touching History*, p 29; Michael D. Doubler, *The National Guard and the War on Terror: The Attacks of 9/11 and Homeland Security* (Washington, D.C.: National Guard Bureau, Office of Public Affairs, Historical Services Division, May 1, 2006), p 22.

36. McFadden, "U.S. Details Careful Plan Of Hijacker," Feb 13, 1993, section 1, *New York Times*, p 23; 9/11 Commission, "[MFR] of the Interview with James Fox of NEADS Conducted by Team 8, 10/29/2003," RG 148: Records of Commissions of the Legislative Branch, 1928–2006, Center for Legislative Archives, NARA, Washington, D.C.

37. 9/11 Commission undated, unsigned miscellaneous working papers: information on Lufthansa Airlines Flight 592 and American Airlines Flight 11.

38. 9/11 Commission, "[MFR] of the Interview of Joe McCain of the NEADS Conducted by Team 8, 10/28/2003" [interview continued on 01/20/2004], RG 148: Records of Commissions of the Legislative Branch, 1928–2006, Center for Legislative Archives, NARA, Washington, D.C. [http://media.nara.gov/9-11/MFR/t-0148-911MFR-00761.pdf, accessed Feb 3, 2009.]

39. Spencer, *Touching History*, p 26.

40. Chairman of the Joint Chiefs of Staff Instruction, "Aircraft Piracy (Hijacking) and Destruction of Derelict Airborne Objects," CJCSI 3610.01A, Jun 1, 2001. [http://www.dtic.mil/doctrine/jel/cjcsd/cjcsi/3610_01a.pdf, accessed Aug 19, 2008.] This instruction cancelled an earlier, same-titled instruction, CJCSI 3610.01, Jul 31, 1997.

41. Federal Aviation Administration order, "Special Military Operations," Order 7610.4J, effective Nov 3, 1998; includes changes effective Jul 3, 2000, and Jul 12, 2001: Chapter 7. Escort of Hijacked Aircraft, Section 1. General, Paragraph 7-1-1. Purpose. [http://web.archive.org/web/20011122232504/www.faa.gov/ATpubs/MIL/Ch7/mil0701.html, accessed Apr 1, 2009.]

42. Ibid., Ch. 7., § 1., Para. 7-1-1., Subparas. a., b., and c.; and Para. 7-1-2. Requests for Service.

43. Federal Aviation Administration order, "Air Traffic Control," Order 7110.65M, effective Oct 28, 1999; includes change effective Jul 12, 2001: Chapter 10. Emergencies. Direct quotes from Section 1. General, Paragraph 10-1-3. Providing Assistance. [http://web.archive.org/web/20010710181612/www.faa.gov/ATpubs/ATC/Chp10/atc1001.html, accessed Apr 1, 2001]; Section 2. Emergency Assistance, Paragraph 10-2-1. Information Requirements; Paragraph 10-2-5. Emergency Situations; and Paragraph 10-2-6. Hijacked Aircraft. [http://web.archive.org/web/20010820151925/www.faa.gov/ATpubs/ATC/Chp10/atc1002.html, accessed Apr 1, 2009.]

44. As CJCSI 3610.01A of Jun 1, 2001, in particular made clear, the chains of command were lengthy. Information about a confirmed hijacking and any request from the FAA for military assistance from NORAD had to pass through several layers of notification and approval, from the air traffic control level up to and down from the office of the secretary of defense. *The 9/11 Commission Final Report*, pp 17 and 18 and p 458, endnote 102, citing, e.g., FAA report, "Crisis Management Handbook for Significant Events," Feb 15, 2000. FAA Order 7110.65M, effective Oct 28, 1999: Ch. 10., § 2. Emergency Assistance, Para. 10-2-6. Hijacked Aircraft. [http://web.archive.org/web/20010820151925/www.faa.gov/ATpubs/ATC/Chp10/atc1002.html, accessed Apr 1, 2009]; 9/11 Commission, "[MFR] of the Interview of Terry Biggio of the Federal Aviation Administration Conducted by Team 8, 09/22/2003," RG 148: Records of Commissions of the Legislative Branch, 1928–2006, Center for Legislative Archives, NARA, Washington, D.C. [http://media.nara.gov/9-11/MFR/t-0148-911MFR-01

153.pdf, accessed Jan 27, 2009.]

45. 9/11 Commission, "[MFR] of an Interview with Paul Worcester of the United States Air Force Conducted by Team 8, 10/14/2003," RG 148: Records of Commissions of the Legislative Branch, 1928–2006, Center for Legislative Archives, NARA, Washington, D.C. [http://media.nara.gov/9-11/MFR/t-0148-911MFR-00914.pdf, accessed Oct 27, 2009.]

46. 9/11 Commission MFRs, including "[MFR] of the Interview of Jeffrey Philips of the Federal Aviation Administration Conducted by Team 8, 09/25/2003," RG 148: Records of Commissions of the Legislative Branch, 1928–2006, Center for Legislative Archives, NARA, Washington, D.C. [http://media.nara.gov/9-11/MFR/t-0148-911MFR-00633.pdf, accessed Feb 4, 2009]; "[MFR] of the Interview of Anthony Schifano of the Federal Aviation Administration Conducted by Team 8, 09/24/2003," RG 148: Records of Commissions of the Legislative Branch, 1928–2006, Center for Legislative Archives, NARA, Washington, D.C. [http://media.nara.gov/9-11/MFR/t-0148-911MFR-006 35.pdf, accessed Feb 5, 2009.]

47. Boston Air Route Traffic Control Center (ARTCC) traffic management unit supervisor Daniel D. Bueno, an almost 20-year FAA veteran, recalled that before 9/11, he had never trained for a scenario involving a NORAC [no radio communication] hijack. 9/11 Commission, "[MFR] of the Interview of Daniel D. Bueno of the Federal Aviation Administration Conducted by Team 8, 09/22/2003," RG 148: Records of Commissions of the Legislative Branch, 1928–2007, Center for Legislative Archives, NARA, Washington, D.C. [http://media.nara.gov/9-11/MFR/t-0148-911MFR-01139.pdf, accessed Jan 27, 2009.]

48. 9/11 Commission, "[MFR] of the Interview of William Dean of the Federal Aviation Administration Conducted by Team 8, 09/22/2003," RG 148: Records of Commissions of the Legislative Branch, 1928–2006, Center for Legislative Archives, NARA, Washington, D.C. [http://media.nara.gov/9-11/MFR/t-0148-911MFR-01145.pdf, accessed Jan 30, 2009.]

49. Before the 9/11 attacks, FAA training programs required for air traffic controllers, such as the Dynamic Simulation (DynSim) and computer-based instruction courses (CBI), were predicated on the notion that pilots would be able to communicate with controllers in hijack situations. In fact, in pre-9/11 FAA hijack exercise simulations, pilots were able to inform air traffic controllers of their circumstances by verbally confirming transponder code "7500" for hijackings, "7600" for malfunctioning transponders, and "7700" for emergencies. 9/11 Commission, "[MFR] of the Interview of Toby Miller of the Federal Aviation Administration Conducted by Team 8, 09/22/2003," RG 148: Records of Commissions of the Legislative Branch, 1928–2006, Center for Legislative Archives, NARA, Washington, D.C. [http://media.nara.gov/9-11/MFR/t-0148-911MFR-01144.pdf, accessed Feb 4, 2009]; 9/11 Commission, MFR, Biggio, 09/22/2003, RG 148, NARA, Washington, D.C. In the hijack scenarios included in the annual or twice-a-year courses, air traffic controllers received from pilots the standard hijack code and were not required to determine, through any other means, whether or not a hijack was underway. 9/11 Commission, "[MFR] of the Interview of John Werth of the Cleveland Air Traffic Control Center Conducted by Team 8, 10/01/2003," RG 148: Records of Commissions of the Legislative Branch, 1928–2007, Center for Legislative Archives, NARA, Washington, D.C. [http://media.nara.gov/9-11/MFR/t-0148-911MFR-00158.pdf, accessed Feb 9, 2009.]

50. *The 9/11 Commission Final Report*, pp 4–5 (American Airlines Flight 11), p 7 (United Airlines Flight 175), p 8 (American Airlines Flight 77), and p 11 (United Airlines Flight 93).

51. 9/11 Commission, MFR, Biggio, 09/22/2003, RG 148, NARA, Washington, D.C. Staff at Boston ARTCC, some of whom had USAF experience, disagreed about the applicability of FAA DynSim and CBI hijack training for air traffic controllers to the circumstances of the 9/11 attacks and about whether training scenarios included multiple hijacks and FAA-NORAD intercept procedures. Air traffic control staff at New York ARTCC generally agreed about the inapplicability of FAA hijack training for air traffic controllers to the circumstances of the 9/11 attacks. Pre-9/11 training scenarios were based on the pilot remaining control of the aircraft; in some instances, the pilot might employ a code word or even explain the situation. For Boston ARTCC: 9/11 Commission MFRs, including "[MFR] of the Interview of Shirley Kula of the Federal Aviation Administration Conducted by Team 8, 09/22/2003," RG 148: Records of Commissions of the Legislative Branch, 1928–2006, Center for Legislative Archives, NARA, Washington, D.C. [http://media.nara.gov/9-11/MFR/t-0148-911MFR-01152.pdf, accessed Feb 3, 2009]; MFR, Biggio, 09/22/2003, RG 148, NARA, Washington, D.C.; "[MFR] of the Interview of Richard Beringer of the Federal Aviation Administration Conducted by Team 8, 09/22/2003," RG 148: Records of Commissions of the Legislative Branch, 1928–2006, Cen-

ter for Legislative Archives, NARA, Washington, D.C. [http://media.nara.gov/9-11/MFR/t-0148-911MFR-01141.pdf, accessed Jan 27, 2009.] For New York ARTCC: 9/11 Commission MFRs, including "[MFR] of the Interview of Charles Alfaro of the Federal Aviation Administration Conducted by Team 8, 09/30/2003," RG 148: Records of Commissions of the Legislative Branch, 1928–2006, Center for Legislative Archives, NARA, Washington, D.C. [http://media.nara.gov/9-11/MFR/t-0148-911MFR-01163.pdf, accessed Jan 26, 2009]; "[MFR] of the Interview of Lorraine Barrett of the Federal Aviation Administration Conducted by Team 8, 10/01/2003," RG 148: Records of Commissions of the Legislative Branch, 1928–2006, Center for Legislative Archives, NARA, Washington, D.C. [http://media.nara.gov/9-11/MFR/t-0148-911MFR-01174.pdf, accessed Jan 27, 2009.]

52. 9/11 Commission, "[MFR] of the Interview of Steven Roebuck of the Federal Aviation Administration Conducted by Team 8, 09/22/2003," RG 148: Records of Commissions of the Legislative Branch, 1928–2007, Center for Legislative Archives, NARA, Washington, D.C. [http://media.nara.gov/9-11/MFR/t-0148-911MFR-01143.pdf, accessed Feb 5, 2009.]

53. Ibid.

54. 9/11 Commission, MFR, Beringer, 09/22/2003, RG 148, NARA, Washington, D.C. Mr. Rosenberg, one of the longest serving FAA employees on 9/11 and one of the traffic management unit supervisors at New York ARTCC on the morning of 9/11, had worked as a USAF air traffic controller before becoming an FAA controller in 1969. 9/11 Commission, "[MFR] of the Interview of Rosenberg [no first name indicated] of the Federal Aviation Administration Conducted by Team 8, 10/01/2003," RG 148: Records of Commissions of the Legislative Branch, 1928–2007, Center for Legislative Archives, NARA, Washington, D.C. [http://media.nara.gov/9-11/MFR/t-0148-911MFR-01168.pdf, accessed Feb 5, 2009.]

55. Boston ARTCC traffic management unit supervisor Daniel D. Bueno, an FAA veteran of almost 20 years, recalled that before 9/11, there had not been such a joint FAA-NORAD simulation or exercise. 9/11 Commission, MFR, Bueno, 09/22/2003, RG 148, NARA, Washington, D.C. But Boston ARTCC military operations specialist Colin Scoggins, a former F–4 crew chief, believed that a joint FAA/military exercise conducted " in 1995 or 1996 . . . involved a military scramble to escort a hijacked aircraft, and the fighter was unable to intercept." 9/11 Commission, "[MFR] of the Interview of Collin [sic] Scoggins of the Federal Aviation Administration Conducted by Team 8, 09/22/2003," RG 148: Records of Commissions of the Legislative Branch, 1928–2007, Center for Legislative Archives, NARA, Washington, D.C. [http://media.nara.gov/9-11/MFR/t-0148-911MFR-01147.pdf, accessed Feb 5, 2009.]

56. Richard Byard, a 17-year veteran air traffic controller and controller in charge at the Indianapolis ARTCC on 9/11, had, in the years before the attacks, participated in annual training-simulator exercises involving hijack situations. In none of the exercises did Byard encounter a suicide hijacker. 9/11 Commission, "[MFR] of the Interview of Richard Byard of the Federal Aviation Administration Conducted by Team 8, 09/24/2003," RG 148: Records of Commissions of the Legislative Branch, 1928–2006, Center for Legislative Archives, NARA, Washington, D.C. [http://media.nara.gov/9-11/MFR/t-0148-911MFR-00628.pdf, accessed Jan 27, 2009.] According to John Werth, a 30-year veteran air traffic controller at the Cleveland ARTCC on 9/11 who was briefly involved in the search for United Airlines Flight 175 and American Airlines Flight 77, and who handled both Delta Airlines Flight 1989 and United Airlines Flight 93, FAA training exercises did not prepare controllers for multiple hijackings or for suicide hijackings, and no one ever discussed such a scenario or possibility. 9/11 Commission, MFR, Werth, 10/01/2003, RG 148, NARA, Washington, D.C.

57. *Staff Monograph*, Part II, p 53.

58. Ibid., p 53, directly quoting FAA briefing, Office of Civil Aviation Security, "The Transnational Threat to Civil Aviation," 2001 CD-ROM Terrorism Threat Presentation to Aviation Security Personnel at Airports and Air Carriers, Slide 24. See *Staff Monograph*, Part II, p 102, endnote 424.

59. *The 9/11 Commission Final Report*, p 264 and p 535, endnote 47, citing Slide 24 of the FAA briefing listed in endnote 58. [http://govinfo.library.unt.edu/911/report/911Report_Ch8.pdf, accessed Sep 29, 2009.]

60. Quotes from 9/11 Commission, "[MFR] of the Interview of Don Dillman of American Airlines Conducted by Team 8, 11/18/2003," RG 148: Records of Commissions of the Legislative Branch, 1928–2006, Center for Legislative Archives, NARA, Washington, D.C. [http://media.nara.gov/9-11/MFR/t-0148-911MFR-00008.pdf, accessed Feb 2, 2009.]

61. FAA Order 7110.65M, effective Oct 28, 1999; Ch. 10., § 1. General, Para. 10-1-1. Emer-

66

gency Determinations, Subpara. c.

62. Ibid., Ch. 10., § 1. General, Para. 10-1-2. Obtaining Information and § 2. Emergency Assistance, Para. 10-2-6. Hijacked Aircraft.

63. Ibid., Ch. 10., § 2. Emergency Assistance, Para. 10-2-1. Information Requirements, Subpara. a.

64. John Werth, directly quoted in 9/11 Commission, MFR, Werth, 10/01/2003, RG 148, NARA, Washington, D.C.

65. *The 9/11 Commission Final Report*, p 16 and p 457, endnote 95. 9/11 Commission MFRs, including "[MFR] of the Staff Visit to Boston [Air Route Traffic Control] Center [Nashua, N.H.], New England Region [Burlington, Mass.], of the Federal Aviation Administration (FAA) Conducted by Team 8, 09/22[– 24] /2003," RG 148: Records of Commissions of the Legislative Branch, 1928–2006, Center for Legislative Archives, NARA, Washington, D.C. [http://media.nara.gov/9-11/MFR/t-0148-911MFR-01154.pdf, accessed Feb 6, 2009]; MFR, Werth, 10/01/2003, RG 148, NARA, Washington, D.C.; MFR, Biggio, 09/22/2003, RG 148, NARA, Washington, D.C.; "[MFR] of the Interview of Mark Merced of the Federal Aviation Administration Conducted by Team 8, 10/01/2003," RG 148: Records of Commissions of the Legislative Branch, 1928–2006, Center for Legislative Archives, NARA, Washington, D.C. [http://media.nara.gov/9-11/MFR/t-0148-911MFR-01167.pdf, accessed Feb 4, 2009]; MFR, Alfaro, 09/30/2003, RG 148, NARA, Washington, D.C.; "[MFR] of the Interview of Kevin Delaney of the Federal Aviation Administration Conducted by Team 8, 09/30/2003," RG 148: Records of Commissions of the Legislative Branch, 1928–2006, Center for Legislative Archives, NARA, Washington, D.C. [http://media.nara.gov/9-11/MFR/t-0148-911MFR-01166.pdf, accessed Jan 30, 2009.]

66. FAA Order 7110.65M, effective Oct 28, 1999, Ch. 10., § 2. Emergency Assistance, Para. 10-2-6. Hijacked Aircraft, Subpara. b. 9/11 Commission MFRs, including MFR, Philips, 09/25/2003, RG 148, NARA, Washington, D.C.; MFR, Schifano, 09/24/2003, NARA, Washington, D.C.; "[MFR] of the Interview of Randy Kath of the Federal Aviation Administration Conducted by Team 8, 09/25/2003," RG 148: Records of Commissions of the Legislative Branch, 1928–2006, Center for Legislative Archives, NARA, Washington, D.C. [http://media.nara.gov/9-11/MFR/t-0148-911MFR-00630.pdf, accessed Feb 3, 2009]; MFR, Alfaro, RG 148, NARA, Washington, D.C.

67. *The 9/11 Commission Final Report*, p 458, endnote 102, citing, e.g., David Bottiglia interview (Oct 1, 2003) and FAA report, "Crisis Management Handbook for Significant Events," Feb 15, 2000. 9/11 Commission, MFR, Alfaro, 09/30/2003, RG 148, NARA, Washington, D.C.

68. *The 9/11 Commission Final Report*, p 18 and p 458, endnote 103, citing FAA regulations, DOD memo, CJCS instruction.

69. Ibid., p 18 and p 458, endnote 104, citing, e.g., Ralph Eberhart interview (Mar 1, 2004); Alan Scott interview (Feb 4, 2004); Robert Marr interview (Jan 23, 2004).

70. FAA Order 7610.4J, effective Nov 3, 1998, Ch. 7. Escort of Hijacked Aircraft, § 2. Escort Procedures, Para. 7-2-3. Vectors. [http://web.archive.org/web/20011122233153/www.faa.gov/ATpubs/MIL/Ch7/mil0702.html, accessed Apr 1, 2009.]

71. *The 9/11 Commission Final Report*, p 18.

72. Kean and Hamilton, *Without Precedent*, pp 265, 267.

73. Miles Kara, a retired U.S. Army colonel and former 9/11 Commission Team 8 staff member, pointed out the military aspects of the 9/11 attacks in his fine research paper, "A Framework for Analysis," article on his 9-11 Revisited website, n.d. [http://www.oredigger61.org/?page_id=10, accessed Sep 30, 2009.]

74. *The 9/11 Commission Final Report*, pp 20 and 21, and p 458, particularly endnotes 115 and 116, citing FAA memo, "Full Transcript; Aircraft Accident; AAL11; New York, NY; September 11, 2001," Apr 19, 2002, p 5, and FAA and NEADS interviews. Bronner, "9/11 Live: The NORAD Tapes," *Vanity Fair*, Aug 2006.

75. Federal Aviation Administration, FAA Registry, Aircraft, N-Number Inquiry Results: N334AA [American Airlines Flight 11]. [http://registry.faa.gov/aircraftinquiry/NNum_Results.aspx?NNumbertxt=334AA, accessed Sep 29, 2009, brought to author's attention by Mike Williams (of 911myths.com) e-mail to P. D. Jones, Sep 29, 2009, 1:04 p.m. EDT.] Don Dillman of American Airlines told 9/11 Commission staffers that American Airlines Flight 11 was a Boeing 767-200. 9/11 Commission, MFR, Dillman, 11/18//2003, RG 148, NARA, Washington, D.C.

76. *The 9/11 Commission Final Report*, p 4 and p 452, endnotes 22–24, citing, e.g., American Airlines documents, 9/11 Commission analysis of NTSB and FAA air traffic control and radar data, and

NTSB reports on air traffic control recordings.

77. American Airlines Flight 11 took a 20-degree turn as instructed. 9/11 Commission, MFR, Kula, 09/22/2003, RG 148, NARA, Washington, D.C.

78. This section is based on *The 9/11 Commission Final Report*, pp 18–20, and p 458, endnotes 106 and 107, citing interviews of Boston ARTCC staffers Peter Zalewski, Terry Biggio, Collin Scoggins, and Daniel Bueno; and FAA memo, "Full Transcript; Aircraft Accident; AAL11; New York, NY; September 11, 2001," Apr 19, 2002.

79. The "guard" frequency was an open emergency frequency "used for the entire Boston Center airspace." Direct quote from 9/11 Commission, MFR, Kula, 09/22/2003, RG 148, NARA, Washington, D.C.

80. Peter Zalewski and several of his Boston Center colleagues later told 9/11 Commission staffers that American Airlines Flight 11 was actually a "NORAC"—not "NORDO"—aircraft. A pilot of a NORDO aircraft was in control of the plane but was unable, perhaps because of malfunctioning radio equipment or other technical reason, to communicate with air traffic controllers. A pilot of a NORAC ("no radio communication") aircraft had a working radio but was deliberately not communicating with controllers. 9/11 Commission, "[MFR] of the Interview of Peter Zalewski of the Federal Aviation Administration Conducted by Team 8, 09/22/2003," RG 148: Records of Commissions of the Legislative Branch, 1928–2006, Center for Legislative Archives, NARA, Washington, D.C. [http://media.nara.gov/9-11/MFR/t-0148-911MFR-01150.pdf, accessed Feb 9, 2009]; 9/11 Commission, MFR, Staff Visit to Boston Center, 09/22/2003, RG 148, NARA, Washington, D.C.

81. 9/11 Commission MFRs: Zalewski, 09/22/2003, and Schifano, 09/24/2003, both RG 148, NARA, Washington, D.C. Shirley Kula, a Boston Center air traffic controller supervisor working a radar associate position on 9/11, told 9/11 Commission staff that "it was usual to have a NORAC (no radio communication) airplane in that sector." 9/11 Commission, MFR, Kula, 09/22/2003, RG 148, NARA, Washington, D.C.

82. Department of Transportation, Federal Aviation Administration, "Report of Aircraft Accident," Report No. ZBW-ARTCC-148, Report Date: Nov 13, 2001; Aircraft Type and Identification: Boeing 767-200 (B762), AAL11; Date/Time of Accident (GMT): Sep 11, 2001, 1246 UTC. The National Security Archive, The September 11th Sourcebooks, NSAEBB No. 165, posted Sep 9, 2005, Document 6. [http://www.gwu.edu/~nsarchiv/NSAEBB/NSAEBB165/faa6.pdf, accessed Apr 29, 2008]; 9/11 Commission MFRs: MFR, Zalewski, 09/22/2003, RG 148, NARA, Washington, D.C.; "[MFR] of the Interview of Brazilino Martens [spelled Martins in DOT, FAA, "Report of Aircraft Accident," Report No. ZBW-ARTCC-148, Report Date: Nov 13, 2001] of the Federal Aviation Administration Conducted by Team 8, 09/22/2003," RG 148: Records of Commissions of the Legislative Branch, 1928–2006, Center for Legislative Archives, NARA, Washington, D.C. [http://media.nara.gov/9-11/MFR/t-0148-911MFR-01155.pdf, accessed Feb 3, 2009]; MFR, Kula, 09/22/2003, RG 148, NARA, Washington, D.C.; MFR, Beringer, 09/22/2003, NARA, Washington, D.C.

83. 9/11 Commission, unmarked, undated draft chapter 7, "A New Kind of War: The Four Flights, the Attacks, and the Defense of the Homeland on September 11," [pp 7–9], RG 148: Records of Commissions of the Legislative Branch, Center for Legislative Archives, NARA, Washington, D.C., citing transcript, ZBW-ARTCC-148, 20R, at 5-7 and 6-7; 9/11 Commission, "[MFR] of the Interview of John Hartling of the Federal Aviation Administration Conducted by Team 8, 09/22/2003," RG 148: Records of Commissions of the Legislative Branch, 1928–2007, Center for Legislative Archives, NARA, Washington, D.C. [http://media.nara.gov/9-11/MFR/t-0148-911MFR-01138.pdf, accessed Feb 2, 2009]; U.S. Department of Transportation, Federal Aviation Administration, Lucius V. Free, Support Specialist, Training/Quality Assurance, Boston ARTCC, Memorandum, ZBW [Boston]-ARTCC-148, AAL11, subj: Information: Full Transcript; Aircraft Accident; AAL11; New York, NY; September 11, 2001; from Boston ARTCC to Aircraft Accident File ZBW-ARTCC-148, Jan 28, 2002, attaching transcript covering the Boston ARTCC Kingston Sector, Sector 20, Radar Position [John Hartling] from 1231–1244 UTC, Sep 11, 2001. Information from transcript at 1237:40 (U.S. Air Flight 583) and 1238:05 (United Airlines Flight 175) UTC [8:37:40 and 8:38:05 a.m. EDT]. [http://www.scribd.com/doc/14142132/T8-B3-Boston-Center-John-Hartling-Fdr-Transcript-Boston-ARTCC-Kingston-Sector-20-Radar-Position-12311244-UTC-Pgs-211-of-11-Total-in-File, accessed Jul, 20, 2009.]

84. According to the FAA, the final transponder return from American Airlines Flight 11 was at 1220:48 UTC (8:20:48 EDT). Coordinated Universal Time (UTC), the international time standard, is the current term for what was commonly referred to as Greenwich Mean Time (GMT). On Sep 11,

2001, UTC time was four hours ahead of Eastern Daylight Time. The 9/11 Commission rounded up that time to 8:21 a.m. EDT. DOT, FAA, "Report of Aircraft Accident," AAL11; Date/Time of Accident (GMT): Sep 11, 2001, 1246 UTC. The National Security Archive, The September 11th Sourcebooks, NSAEBB No. 165, Doc 6. *The 9/11 Commission Final Report*, p 18.

85. DOT, FAA, "Report of Aircraft Accident," AAL11; Date/Time of Accident (GMT): Sep 11, 2001, 1246 UTC. The National Security Archive, The September 11th Sourcebooks, NSAEBB No. 165, Doc 6; DOT, FAA, "Summary of Air Traffic Hijack Events, September 11, 2001," The National Security Archive, The September 11th Sourcebooks, NSAEBB No. 165, Doc 7; *The 9/11 Commission Final Report*, pp 16, 18; 9/11 Commission, MFR, Martens, 09/22/2003, RG 148, NARA, Washington, D.C.; Don Phillips, "Radar screen blip raised suspicions[: Unidentified jet's transponder had been deactivated]," *Washington Post*, Sep 12, 2001. [http://www.chicagotribune.com/news/nationworld/chi-0109120177sep12,0,6023488.story, accessed Apr 23, 2009.]

86. Because the primary target had been tagged, "the data block of the last known information stayed with the primary." 9/11 Commission, "[MFR] of the Interview of Joseph Cooper of the Federal Aviation Administration Conducted by Team 8, 09/22/2003," RG 148: Records of Commissions of the Legislative Branch, 1928–2006, Center for Legislative Archives, NARA, Washington, D.C. [http://media.nara.gov/9-11/MFR/t-0148-911MFR-01140.pdf, accessed Jan 30, 2009.] It is unclear whether Boston Center controllers manually, or their computers automatically, gave a data tag to the American Airlines Flight 11 primary target. 9/11 Commission MFRs: Zalewski, 09/22/2003, and Dean, 09/22/2003, both RG 148, NARA, Washington, D.C. In any event, AAL 11 "received a flight data tag and was under primary tracking" while it was still in the center's Area C airspace. 9/11 Commission, "[MFR] of the Interview of Alan Miller of the Federal Aviation Administration Conducted by Team 8, 09/22/2003," RG 148: Records of Commissions of the Legislative Branch, 1928–2007, Center for Legislative Archives, NARA, Washington, D.C. [http://media.nara.gov/9-11/MFR/t-0148-911MFR-01137.pdf, accessed Feb 4, 2009.]

87. Bronner, "9/11 Live: The NORAD Tapes," Aug 2006.

88. "Radar shows plane headed straight for Pentagon," *USA Today*, Associated Press, Sep 21, 2001, updated 12:38 p.m. ET [probably EDT]. [http://www.usatoday.com/news/nation/2001/09/21/plane-pentagon.htm, accessed Apr 24, 2009]; Matthew L. Wald, "Controllers Say Flow of Information on Hijacked Planes' Course Was Slow and Uneven," *New York Times*, Sep 13, 2001. [http://www.nytimes.com/2001/09/13/national/13AVIA.html?pagewanted=print, accessed May 13, 2009.]

89. Despite Kevin Delaney's experience in the military operations specialist position at New York ARTCC during Desert Storm (1990–1991), "he was not aware that certain military radar facilities could read altitude on a primary target." 9/11 Commission, MFR, Delaney, 09/30/2003, RG 148, NARA, Washington, D.C.

90. Bronner, "9/11 Live: The NORAD Tapes," Aug 2006. "Transcripts from Voice Recorder, 11 September 2001, 1227Z–1417Z, Northeast Air Defense Sector (NEADS), Rome, NY," DRM 1, Dat 2, Channel 4 ID1—OP Position. [http://www.scribd.com/doc/18664001/T8-B20-NEADS-Trip-2-of-3-Fdr-Transcript-NEADS-Rome-NY-DRM-2-Dat-2-Pg-183-ColorCoded, accessed Oct 7, 2009.]

91. *Staff Monograph on the Four Flights and Civil Aviation Security*, 9/11 Commission Staff Report dated Aug 26, 2004, 2d version, Part I: "The Four Flights," (hereinafter *Staff Monograph*, Part I), p 10. [http://www.archives.gov/legislative/research/9-11/staff-report-sept2005.pdf, accessed Mar 3, 2008.]

92. *The 9/11 Commission Final Report*, pp 18–19 and p 458, endnotes 107 and 108, citing DOD radar files, 84th Radar Evaluation Squadron, "9/11 Autoplay," n.d.; Peter Zalewski and John Schippani interviews (Sep 22, 2003).

93. U.S. Department of Transportation, Federal Aviation Administration, Karen L. Goff, Quality Assurance Technician, Boston ARTCC, Memorandum, ZBW [Boston]-ARTCC-148, AAL11, subj: Information: Full Transcript; Aircraft Accident; AAL11; New York, NY; September 11, 2001; from Boston ARTCC to Aircraft Accident File ZBW-ARTCC-148, Feb 15, 2002, attaching transcript covering the Boston ARTCC Boston Sector, Sector 46, Radar Position [Peter Zalewski] from 1204–1240 UTC, Sep 11, 2001. Direct quote from transcript. [http://www.scribd.com/doc/13950352/T8-B3-Boston-Center-Peter-Zalewski-Fdr-ARTCC-Transcript-Sector-46-Re-AA-11-We-Have-Some-Planes, accessed Oct 6, 2009.]

94. *Staff Monograph*, Part I, p 10.

95. DOT, FAA, Goff, Memorandum, ZBW [Boston]-ARTCC-148, AAL11, attaching transcript

covering ZBW Boston Sector, Sector 46, Radar Position [Zalewski] from 1204–1240 UTC, Sep 11, 2001. Direct quote from transcript.

96. Ritter, "Flight Path Study—American Airlines Flight 11," Feb 19, 2002, NTSB. The National Security Archive, The September 11th Sourcebooks, NSAEBB No. 196, Doc 1.

97. DOT, FAA, Goff, Memorandum, ZBW [Boston]-ARTCC-148, AAL11, attaching transcript covering ZBW Boston Sector, Sector 46, Radar Position [Zalewski] from 1204–1240 UTC, Sep 11, 2001. Direct quote from transcript.

98. *The 9/11 Commission Final Report*, p 6.

99. The descent, which began at 8:37:30 a.m. EDT, was flown at an average rate of about 3,200 feet/minute. Ritter, "Flight Path Study—American Airlines Flight 11," Feb 19, 2002, NTSB. The National Security Archive, The September 11th Sourcebooks, NSAEBB No. 196, Doc 1.

100. During a twenty-five-minute call to personnel at the American Airlines Southeastern Reservations Office in Cary, N.C., Flight 11 coach cabin attendant Betty Ong said that no announcements were made over the plane's public address system. Federal Bureau of Investigation, memorandum from Charlotte [N.C.], Raleigh Resident Agency, to Director's Office, Attn: SIOC, dated Sep 13, 2001. Federal Bureau of Investigation, FD-302s reflecting interview of Vanessa Dias Minter, dated and transcribed Sep 12, 2001; and of Michael Woodward, dated Sep 11, 2001, transcribed Sep 12, 2001. [All: http://www.scribd.com/doc/24393263/T7-B13-Flight-Call-Notes-and-302s-Folder-Entire-Contents, accessed Jan 4, 2010.]

101. *Staff Monograph*, Part I, p 10; *The 9/11 Commission Final Report*, p 6.

102. Direct quote from transcript of aircraft-ground communication from takeoff to accident time on Sep 11, 2001, in Joseph A. Gregor, "Specialist's Report," Air Traffic Control Recording: United Airlines Flight 175, Dec 21, 2001. National Transportation Safety Board, Vehicle Recorders Division, Washington, D.C. The National Security Archive, The September 11th Sourcebooks, NSAEBB No. 196, posted Aug 11, 2006, Document 7. [http://www.gwu.edu/~nsarchiv/NSAEBB/NSAEBB196/doc07.pdf, accessed Apr 30, 2008.] At 8:42 a.m. EDT, Bottiglia passed the information from United Airlines Flight 175 to Boston Center radar associate William Dean. DOT, FAA, "Report of Aircraft Accident," AAL11; Date/Time of Accident (GMT): Sep 11, 2001, 1246 UTC, The National Security Archive, The September 11th Sourcebooks, NSAEBB No. 165, Doc 6. 9/11 Commission, "[MFR] of the Interview of David Bottiglia of the Federal Aviation Administration Conducted by Team 8, 10/01/2003," RG 148: Records of Commissions of the Legislative Branch, 1928–2007, Center for Legislative Archives, NARA, Washington, D.C. [http://media.nara.gov/9-11/MFR/t-0148-911MFR-01171.pdf, accessed Jan 27, 2009]; *The 9/11 Commission Final Report*, pp 7, 21, p 454, and 459, endnotes 42 and 122.

103. *Staff Monograph*, Part I, p 10; 9/11 Commission, MFR, Zalewski, 09/22/2003, RG 148, NARA, Washington, D.C.

104. *The 9/11 Commission Final Report*, p 19; 9/11 Commission, "[MFR] of the Interview of Robert Jones of the Federal Aviation Administration Conducted by Team 8, 09/22/2003," RG 148: Records of Commissions of the Legislative Branch, 1928–2007, Center for Legislative Archives, NARA, Washington, D.C. [http://media.nara.gov/9-11/MFR/t-0148-911MFR-01142.pdf, accessed Feb 3, 2009]; 9/11 Commission, MFR, Biggio, 09/22/2003, RG 148, NARA, Washington, D.C. Biggio's notification to the Regional Operations Center came at about 9:03 a.m., according to the *Staff Monograph*, Part II, p 15, citing Zalewski interview, Sep 23 [sic: 22], 2003.

105. *The 9/11 Commission Final Report*, p 458, endnote 102; 9/11 Commission, MFR, Biggio, 09/22/2003, RG 148, NARA, Washington, D.C.

106. Direct quote from 9/11 Commission, MFR, Staff Visit to Boston Center, 09/22/2003, RG 148, NARA, Washington, D.C. 9/11 Commission, MFR, Bueno, 09/22/2003, RG 148, NARA, Washington, D.C.

107. Personnel Statement, Federal Aviation Administration, Boston ARTCC, ZBW-ARTCC-148, AAL11, Daniel D. Bueno, Sep 11, 2001. [http://www.scribd.com/doc/14142139/T8-B3-Boston-Center-Terry-Biggio-Fdr-Dan-Bueno-FAA-Personnel-Statement-and-Handwritten-Notes, accessed Oct 15, 2009.]

108. At FAA headquarters, for example, the head of Civil Aviation Security Intelligence (ACI) told the Civil Aviation Security Operations (ACO) duty officer at 8:45 a.m. that the Washington Operations Center (WOC) was reporting that American Airlines Flight 11 "may have an intruder in the cockpit." Air traffic controllers had no radio contact with the aircraft, but the "pilot is keying the microphone

and threatening comments are overheard." Federal Aviation Administration (FAA), "Executive Summary Chronology of a Multiple Hijacking Crisis September 11, 2001," Sep 17, 2001. The National Security Archive, The September 11th Sourcebooks, NSAEBB No. 165, posted Sep 9, 2005, Document 5. [http://www.gwu.edu/~nsarchiv/NSAEBB/NSAEBB165/faa5.pdf, accessed Apr 29, 2008.]

109. 9/11 Commission, [MFR] of the Interview of Robert C. McLaughlin of the Federal Aviation Administration Conducted by Team 7, 06/03/2004," RG 148: Records of Commissions of the Legislative Branch, 1928–2007, Center for Legislative Archives, NARA, Washington, D.C. [http://media.nara.gov/9-11/MFR/t-0148-911MFR-00717.pdf, accessed Feb 3, 2009.]

110. Department of Transportation, Federal Aviation Administration, "Chronology [FAA Headquarters] ADA-30 [McKie], Operations Center: Terrorist Attacks NY-DC 9/11/01." The National Security Archive, The September 11th Sourcebooks, NSAEBB No. 165, posted Sep 9, 2005, Document 1. [http://www.gwu.edu/~nsarchiv/NSAEBB/NSAEBB165/faa1.pdf, accessed Dec 13, 2007]; Department of Transportation, Federal Aviation Administration, New England Regional Operations Center daily log, Sep 11, 2001. The National Security Archive, The September 11th Sourcebooks, NSAEBB No. 165, posted Sep 9, 2005, Document 2. [http://www.gwu.edu/~nsarchiv/NSAEBB/NSAEBB165/faa2.pdf, accessed Dec 13, 2007.]

111. Mark Clayton, "Controllers' Tale of Flight 11," *Christian Science Monitor*, Sep 13, 2001. [http://www.csmonitor.com/2001/0913/p1s2-usju.html, accessed Apr 30, 2008]; Eric Lichtblau, "Aboard Flight 11, a Chilling Voice," *Los Angeles Times*, latimes.com, Sep 20, 2001. [http://web.archive.org/web/20010929230742/http://latimes.com/news/nationworld/nation/la-092001hijack.story, accessed Feb 20, 2009.]

112. 9/11 Commission, MFR, Toby Miller, 09/22/2003, RG 148, NARA, Washington, D.C.

113. 9/11 Commission MFRs: Jones, 09/22/2003, and Staff Visit to Boston Center, 09/22/2003, both RG 148, NARA, Washington, D.C.

114. "Transcripts from Voice Recorder, 11 September 2001, 1227Z–1417Z, Northeast Air Defense Sector (NEADS), Rome, NY," DRM 2, Dat 2, Channel 15 [AST: air surveillance technician]. 13:03:07 [9:03:07 a.m. EDT], 13:04:30–13:04:58 [9:04:30–9:04:58 a.m. EDT], with direct quote at 13:04:58 [9:04:58 a.m. EDT]. [http://www.scribd.com/doc/18664001/T8-B20-NEADS-Trip-2-of-3-Fdr-Transcript-NEADS-Rome-NY-DRM-2-Dat-2-Pg-183-ColorCoded, accessed Oct 7, 2009.]

115. 9/11 Commission, MFR, Bueno, 09/22/2003, RG 148, NARA, Washington, D.C.

116. DOT, FAA, "Report of Aircraft Accident," AAL11; Date/Time of Accident (GMT): Sep 11, 2001, 1246 UTC. The National Security Archive, The September 11th Sourcebooks, NSAEBB No. 165, Doc 6.

117. 9/11 Commission, [MFR] of the Interview of Jon Schippani of the Federal Aviation Administration Conducted by Team 8, 09/22/2003," RG 148: Records of Commissions of the Legislative Branch, 1928–2007, Center for Legislative Archives, NARA, Washington, D.C. [http://media.nara.gov/9-11/MFR/t-0148-911MFR-01149.pdf, accessed Feb 5, 2009]; 9/11 Commission, MFR, Bottiglia, 10/01/2003, RG 148, NARA, Washington, D.C.

118. 9/11 Commission, MFR, Staff Visit to Boston Center, 09/22/2003, RG 148, NARA, Washington, D.C.

119. 9/11 Commission, MFR, Alfaro, 09/30/2003, RG 148, NARA, Washington, D.C.

120. 9/11 Commission MFRs: Bueno, 09/22/2003, and Biggio, 09/22/2003, both RG 148, NARA, Washington, D.C.; and "[MFR] of Site visit [sic] to FAA to listen to audio of the Federal Aviation Administration Conducted by Team 8, 06/12/2003," RG 148: Records of Commissions of the Legislative Branch, 1928–2007, Center for Legislative Archives, NARA, Washington, D.C. [http://media.nara.gov/9-11/MFR/t-0148-911MFR-00243.pdf, accessed Feb 5, 2009]; DOT, FAA, "Summary of Air Traffic Hijack Events, September 11, 2001," The National Security Archive, The September 11th Sourcebooks, NSAEBB No. 165, Doc 7; Personnel Statement, FAA, Boston ARTCC, AAL11, Bueno, Sep 11, 2001; Personnel Statement, Federal Aviation Administration, Boston ARTCC, ZBW-ARTCC-148, AAL11, Terry Biggio, Sep 15, 2001. [http://www.scribd.com/doc/13950370/T8-B3-Boston-Center-Terry-Biggio-Fdr-FAA-Personnel-Statement, accessed Oct 15, 2009.]

121. U.S. Department of Transportation, Federal Aviation Administration, Karen L. Goff, Quality Assurance Technician, Boston ARTCC [Air Route Traffic Control Center], Memorandum, ZBW [Boston]-ARTCC-148, AAL11, subj: Information: Full Transcript; Aircraft Accident; AAL11; New York, NY; September 11, 2001; from Boston ARTCC to Aircraft Accident File ZBW-ARTCC-148, Apr 19, 2002, attaching transcript covering the Boston ARTCC Boston TMU [Traffic Management Unit]

Severe Weather Position [Daniel D. Bueno] from 1222–1250 UTC, Sep 11, 2001. See 1228:45–1229:34 UTC [8:28:45–8:29:34 a.m. EDT]. [http://www.scribd.com/doc/13950333/T8-B3-Boston-Center-Colin-Scoggins-Fdr-ARTCC-Transcript-TMU-Severe-Weather-Position-AA-11, accessed Jul 20, 2009.]

122. *The 9/11 Commission Final Report*, p 19 and p 458, endnotes 111 and 112.

123. Personnel Statement, FAA, Boston ARTCC, AAL11, Bueno, Sep 11, 2001; Personnel Statement, Federal Aviation Administration, Boston ARTCC, ZBW-ARTCC-148, AAL11, Colin Scoggins, Sep 20, 2001. [http://www.scribd.com/doc/13950342/T8-B3-Boston-Center-Colin-Scoggins-Fdr-Chronology-of-Events-and-FAA-Personnel-Statement-Wasnt-in-a-Rush-Went-to-the-Credit-Union-First, accessed Oct 15, 2009]; John Farmer, *The Ground Truth: The Untold Story of America under Attack on 9/11* (New York: Riverhead Books, 2009), p 117; DOT, FAA, Goff, Memorandum, ZBW [Boston]-ARTCC-148, AAL11, Apr 19, 2002, attaching transcript covering the ZBW Boston TMU Severe Weather Position [Bueno] from 1222–1250 UTC, Sep 11, 2001.

124. 9/11 Commission, MFR, Staff Visit to Boston Center, 09/22/2003, RG 148, NARA, Washington, D.C.

125. 9/11 Commission, MFR, Bueno, 09/22/2003, RG 148, NARA, Washington, D.C.

126. This is suggested by DOT, FAA, Goff, Memorandum, ZBW [Boston]-ARTCC-148, AAL11, Apr 19, 2002, attaching transcript covering the ZBW Boston TMU Severe Weather Position [Bueno] from 1222–1250 UTC, Sep 11, 2001: see 1234:33–1234:56 UTC [8:34:33–8:34:56 a.m. EDT].

127. Ibid., direct quotes from transcript, 1235:18 UTC [8:35:18 a.m. EDT] and 1235:14 UTC [8:35:14 a.m. EDT], respectively. Spence made the assurances to Bueno beginning at 1235:24 UTC [8:35:24 a.m. EDT]; Goff's memo and the transcript refer to Cape TRACON as Cape Approach. 9/11 Commission, "[MFR] of Steven Walsh of the Federal Aviation Administration Conducted by Team 8, 09/30/2003," RG 148: Records of Commissions of the Legislative Branch, 1928–2007, Center for Legislative Archives, NARA, Washington, D.C. [http://media.nara.gov/9-11/MFR/t-0148-911MFR-00256.pdf, accessed Feb 9, 2009] and "[MFR] of Tim Spence of the Federal Aviation Administration Conducted by Team 8, 09/30/2003," RG 148: Records of Commissions of the Legislative Branch, 1928–2007, Center for Legislative Archives, NARA, Washington, D.C. [http://media.nara.gov/9-11/MFR/t-0148-911MFR-00254.pdf, accessed Feb 5, 2009]; Personnel Statement, FAA, Boston ARTCC, AAL11, Bueno, Sep 11, 2001.

128. 9/11 Commission, MFR, Walsh, 09/30/2003, RG 148, NARA, Washington, D.C.

129. Filson, *Air War Over America*, p 51. 9/11 Commission MFRs: Marr, 01/23/2004, and Quenneville, 01/07/2004, both RG 148, NARA, Washington, D.C.

130. Spencer, *Touching History*, p 22.

131. Direct quote from Personnel Statement, FAA, Boston ARTCC, AAL11, Scoggins, Sep 20, 2001.

132. Direct quote from 9/11 Commission, MFR, Dean, 09/22/2003, RG 148, NARA, Washington, D.C.

133. Transcribed from audiotape links in Bronner, "9/11 Live: The NORAD Tapes," Aug 2006. See also Transcripts from Voice Recorder, 11 September 2001 1227Z [Zulu or UTC]-1417Z, Northeast Air Defense Sector, Rome, NY, DRM 2, Dat 2, Channel 14, 12:37:24 [8:37:24 a.m. EDT]. [http://www.scribd.com/doc/18664001/T8-B20-NEADS-Trip-2-of-3-Fdr-Transcript-NEADS-Rome-NY-DRM-2-Dat-2-Pg-183-ColorCoded, accessed Oct 7, 2009.] Bronner shows the Cooper-Powell exchange beginning at 8:37:52 a.m. EDT. According to the 9/11 Commission, the NTSB determined that the NEADS clock was 25 seconds slow on the morning of Sep 11. Commission records show the Cooper-Powell exchange beginning at 8:37:52. 9/11 Commission staff excerpts of various transcripts relating to American Airlines Flight 11, n.d. [http://www.scribd.com/doc/18664546/T8-B21-NEADS-Floor-2-of-3-Fdr-Excerpts-From-TapesTranscripts-Re-AA-11-282, accessed Oct 28, 2009]; 9/11 Commission, MFR, Site visit [sic] to FAA to listen to audio, 06/12/2003, RG 148, NARA, Washington, D.C.

134. 9/11 Commission, MFR, McCain, 10/28/2003 [cont'd on 01/20/2004], RG 148, NARA, Washington, D.C.

135. 9/11 Commission MFRs: Cooper, 09/22/2003, and Fox, 10/29/2003, both RG 148, NARA, Washington, D.C.

136. Bronner, "9/11 Live: The NORAD Tapes," Aug 2006; 9/11 Commission, MFR, McCain, 10/28/2003, RG 148, NARA, Washington, D.C.

137. 9/11 Commission, "[MFR] of the Interview of Dawne Deskins of the NEADS Conducted by Team 8, 10/30/2003," RG 148: Records of Commissions of the Legislative Branch, 1928–2006, Center for Legislative Archives, NARA, Washington, D.C. [http://media.nara.gov/9-11/MFR/t-0148-911MFR-00778.pdf, accessed Feb 2, 2009]; Bronner, "9/11 Live: The NORAD Tapes," Aug 2006.

138. "Transcripts from Voice Recorder," 11 Sep 2001, 1227Z–1417Z, NEADS, DRM 1, Dat 2, Channel 4 ID1—OP Position, e.g., at 13:08:23 and 13:09:37 [9:08:23 a.m. and 9:09:37 a.m. EDT].

139. 9/11 Commission, MFR, Deskins, 10/30/2003, RG 148, NARA, Washington, D.C.

140. Direct quotes from "Transcripts from Voice Recorder," 11 Sep 2001, 1227Z–1417Z, NEADS, DRM 2, Dat 2, Channel 14, 12:39:00–12:39:35 [8:39:00–8:39:35 a.m. EDT].

141. Bronner, "9/11 Live: The NORAD Tapes," Aug 2006; 9/11 Commission, MFR, Deskins, 10/30/2003, RG 148, NARA, Washington, D.C.

142. The Otis tower was staffed by contractors, not by military personnel. Spence estimated that he made his calls between 8:36 and 8:40 or 8:41 a.m. 9/11 Commission MFRs: Walsh, 09/30/2003, and Spence, 09/30/2003, both RG 148, NARA, Washington, D.C.

143. Spence did not recall whom he spoke with at the operations desk. 9/11 Commission, MFR, Spence, 09/30/2003, RG 148, NARA, Washington, D.C. Spence was back on the phone with Bueno at 8:43:08 a.m. EDT and told him that Otis required a NEADS authorization; Bueno replied that Boston Center was already working with NEADS personnel to that end. Spence told Bueno seconds later that Panta 45 and 46 would be airborne soon. In the meantime, as Bueno explained to Spence, Boston Center staff had already contacted the NEADS air defenders. DOT, FAA, Goff, Memorandum, ZBW [Boston]-ARTCC-148, AAL11, Apr 19, 2002, attaching transcript covering the ZBW Boston TMU Severe Weather Position [Bueno] from 1222–1250 UTC, Sep 11, 2001: see 1243:08–1243:32 UTC [8:43:08–8:43:32 a.m. EDT].

144. "[Otis] Historian's Report for Sept. 11, 2001, By TSgt Bruce Vittner," n.d. [http://www.scribd.com/doc/13653185/T8-B16-Miles-Kara-Work-Files-Otis-Langley-1-of-2-Fdr-Historians-Report-for-Sept-11-2001-by-TSgt-Bruce-Vittner, accessed Jul 16, 2009.]

145. 9/11 Commission, "[MFR] of an Interview with Michael Kelly of the United States Air Force Conducted by Team 8, 10/14/2003," RG 148: Records of Commissions of the Legislative Branch, 1928–2006, Center for Legislative Archives, NARA, Washington, D.C. [http://media.nara.gov/9-11/MFR/t-0148-911MFR-00912.pdf, accessed Jun 25, 2009.]

146. 9/11 Commission MFRs: Spence, 09/30/2003, and Kelly, 10/14/2003, both RG 148, NARA, Washington, D.C.; Vittner, "[Otis] Historian's Report."

147. 9/11 Commission, MFR, Kelly, 10/14/2003, RG 148, NARA, Washington, D.C.; Spencer, *Touching History*, p 155.

148. 9/11 Commission staff concluded that "According to available transcripts[,] the Cooper call directly to NEADS [Powell] and the Otis tower call [sic: Kelly at Otis Command Center] to NEADS [McCain] based on Bueno's call reached NEADS at nearly the same time, approximately 0838 EDT." Quote from 9/11 Commission, MFR, Staff Visit to Boston Center, 09/22/2003, RG 148, NARA, Washington, D.C. Sources for the times of the Cooper-Powell and Kelly-McCain calls are as follows, respectively: "Transcripts from Voice Recorder," 11 Sep 2001, 1227Z [Zulu or UTC]-1417Z, NEADS, DRM 2, Dat 2, Channel 14, 12:37:24 [8:37:24 a.m. EDT] and DRM 2, Dat 2, Channel 2 MCC-OP, 12:38:15 [8:38:15 a.m. EDT].

149. U.S. Department of Transportation, Federal Aviation Administration, Francis A. Mac-Donald, Jr., Air Traffic Manager, Cape TRACON [Terminal Radar Approach Control], Memorandum, subj: Information: Partial Transcript; Presidential 9/11 Commission Inquiry; from Manager, Cape TRACON, K90-1, to Presidential 9/11 Commission, Oct 10, 2003, attaching transcript covering the Cape TRACON Supervisor[']s position from 1229–1253 UTC, Sep 11, 2001: see 1241: 32 [8:41:32 a.m. EDT]. [http://aal77.com/faa/faa_atc/otis/5%20K90%206%20PARTIAL%20TRANSCRIPTS%203%20POSITIONS%20FLIGHT%20DATA,%20SUPERVISORS%20CONSOLE,%20HIGH%20AR.PDF, accessed Nov 4, 2004.]

150. Direct quote from 9/11 Commission, MFR, Spence, 09/30/2003, RG 148, NARA, Washington, D.C.

151. 9/11 Commission, MFR, Duffy, 01/07/2004, RG 148, NARA, Washington, D.C.; Transcript of intvw, Duffy, Aug 12, 2009, conducted by Johnson, Stewart, and Dysart; Spencer, *Touching History*, pp 27–28; 9/11 Commission, "[MFR]) of an Interview with Daniel S. Nash of the United States Air Force Conducted by Team 8, 10/14/2003," RG 148: Records of Commissions of the Leg-

islative Branch, 1928–2007, Center for Legislative Archives, NARA, Washington, D.C. [http://media.nara.gov/9-11/MFR/t-0148-911MFR-00911.pdf, accessed Nov 10, 2009]; Filson, *Air War Over America*, p 50.

152. Direct quote from transcript of intvw, Duffy, Aug 12, 2009, conducted by Johnson, Stewart, and Dysart. Vittner, "[Otis] Historian's Report."

153. Direct quote from transcript of intvw, Duffy, Aug 12, 2009, conducted by Johnson, Stewart, and Dysart.

154. Ibid.; Vittner, "[Otis] Historian's Report"; Matt Viser, "Two pilots revisit their 9/11," *Boston Globe*, boston.com, Sep 11, 2005 [http://www.boston.com/news/local/Massachusetts/articles/2005/ 09/11/two_pilots_revisit_their_911/, accessed Aug 19, 2008]; Spencer, *Touching History*, pp 28–30.

155. Transcript of intvw, Duffy, Aug 12, 2009, conducted by Johnson, Stewart, and Dysart; Filson, *Air War Over America*, p 50.

156. Direct quote from transcript of intvw, Duffy, Aug 12, 2009, conducted by Johnson, Stewart, and Dysart.

157. 9/11 Commission, MFR, Nash, 10/14/2003, RG 148, NARA, Washington, D.C.; Vittner, "[Otis] Historian's Report"; Viser, "Two pilots revisit their 9/11," Sep 11, 2005.

158. Direct quote from transcript of intvw, Duffy, Aug 12, 2009, conducted by Johnson, Stewart, and Dysart. 9/11 Commission, undated, unsigned transcript of audiotaped intvw, Leslie Filson, with Lt. Col. Tim Duffy, n.d. The transcript is followed by typed notes of Filson's interview with Duffy, Oct 22, 2003. [http://www.scribd.com/doc/18740499/T8-B22-Filson-Materials-Fdr-Lt-Col-Tim-Duffy-Interview-Typed-Notes-321, accessed Jan 7, 2010]; 9/11 Commission, "[MFR] of an Interview with Ng, [FNU] and Stiers, [FNU] of the United States Air Force Conducted by Team 8, 10/14/2003," RG 148: Records of Commissions of the Legislative Branch, 1928–2007, Center for Legislative Archives, NARA, Washington, D.C. [http://media.nara.gov/9-11/MFR/t-0148-911MFR-00913.pdf, accessed Jun 26, 2009.]

159. See sources in endnote 148.

160. 9/11 Commission MFRs: Duffy, 01/07/2004, and Nash, 10/14/2003, both RG 148, NARA, Washington, D.C.; Transcript of intvw, Duffy, Aug 12, 2009, conducted by Johnson, Stewart, and Dysart; Spencer, *Touching History*, pp 27–28; Filson, *Air War Over America*, p 50; Vittner, "[Otis] Historian's Report."

161. Direct quote from 9/11 Commission, MFR, Watson, et al., 10/27/2003 [Marr's initial briefing to 9/11 Commission staff], RG 148, NARA, Washington, D.C.

162. Direct quote from 9/11 Commission, MFR of the interview with Col Randy "Cat" Morris during a CONR field site visit, conducted by Team 8, 02/03/2004. This interview is among those included in 9/11 Commission, "[MFR] of the Interview of Don Arias of the Continental United States North American Aerospace Defense Command Region (CONR) Conducted by Team 8, 02/04/2004," RG 148: Records of Commissions of the Legislative Branch, 1928–2007, Center for Legislative Archives, NARA, Washington, D.C. [http://media.nara.gov/9-11/MFR/t-0148-911MFR-00172.pdf, accessed Jan 21, 2009]; 9/11 Commission, second public hearing, May 22–23, 2003, Washington, D.C., archived website [http://govinfo.library.unt.edu/911/hearings/hearing2.htm, accessed Feb 27, 2008] and Transcript, Panel 1 (Sep 11, 2001: The Attacks and the Response), Day 2 (Civil Aviation Security) [May 23, 2003] of the commission's second public hearing: unsworn testimony of Maj Gen Larry Arnold, USAF (Ret). [http://www.9-11commission.gov/archive/hearing2/9-11Commission_Hearing_2003-05-23.pdf, accessed Jan 18, 2008.]

163. Direct quote from 9/11 Commission, [MFR] of the Interview of Randy Morris of the Air Operations Center (CONR) Conducted by Team 8, 02/02/2004," RG 148: Records of Commissions of the Legislative Branch, 1928–2007, Center for Legislative Archives, NARA, Washington, D.C. [http://media.nara.gov/9-11/MFR/t-0148-911MFR-00173.pdf, accessed Feb 4, 2009.]

164. 9/11 Commission, MFR of the interview with Gen Larry Arnold during a Continental U.S. Region (CONR) field site visit, conducted by Team 8, 02/03/2004. This interview is among those included in 9/11 Commission, MFR, Arias, 02/04/2004, RG 148, NARA, Washington, D.C. 9/11 Commission, second public hearing: transcript, panel 1, day 2 [May 23, 2003], unsworn testimony of Maj Gen Larry Arnold, USAF (Ret); 9/11 Commission, "[MFR] of the Interview of Jim Millovich and Robert Del Toro of the Continental United States Air Defense Region (CONR) Conducted by Team 8, 02/04/2004," RG 148: Records of Commissions of the Legislative Branch, 1928–2007, Center for Leg-

islative Archives, NARA, Washington, D.C. [http://media.nara.gov/9-11/MFR/t-0148-911MFR-00171.pdf, accessed Feb 4, 2009.]

165. Direct quotes from 9/11 Commission, second public hearing: transcript, panel 1, day 2 [May 23, 2003], unsworn testimony of Maj Gen Larry Arnold, USAF (Ret).

166. 9/11 Commission, MFR, Marr, 01/23/2004, RG 148, NARA, Washington, D.C.

167. Vittner, "[Otis] Historian's Report"; Bronner, "9/11 Live: The NORAD Tapes," Aug 2006.

168. After receiving the initial hijack notification from Boston Center, NEADS personnel worked with Boston Center staff to try to locate American Flight 11. They continued to do so before Marr's order to battle stations for the Otis fighters, up to and after Nasypany's scramble order, and, for a time, together with FAA personnel at Boston and New York Centers, even after the doomed flight crashed. 9/11 Commission, "[MFR] of the Interview of Jeremy Powell of the NEADS Conducted by Team 8, 10/27/2003, RG 148: Records of Commissions of the Legislative Branch, 1928–2007, Center for Legislative Archives, NARA, Washington, D.C. [http://media.nara.gov/9-11/MFR/t-0148-911MFR-00768.pdf, accessed Feb 5, 2009]; "Transcripts from Voice Recorder," 11 Sep 2001, 1227Z–1417Z, NEADS, DRM 1, Dat 2, Channel 4 ID1—OP Position: see 12:46:59–12:53:44 [8:46:59–8:53:44 a.m. EDT].

169. Direct quote from 9/11 Commission, MFR, Arnold, 02/03/2004, NARA, Washington, D.C. Filson, *Air War Over America*, p 56. Leslie Filson, handwritten notes of her interview of Robert Marr, n.d. [http://www.scribd.com/doc/18740474/T8-B22-Filson-Materials-Fdr-Col-Bob-Marr-Interview-Handwritten-Notes.]

170. If, however, "the fighters had had a track, then Marr would have expected Nasypany to look to the Battle Cab for direction." Direct quotes from 9/11 Commission, MFR, Marr, 01/23/2004, RG 148, NARA, Washington, D.C.

171. "Transcripts from Voice Recorder," 11 Sep 2001, 1227Z–1417Z, NEADS, DRM 2, Dat 2, Channel 2 MCC-OP, 12:45:00 [8:45:00 a.m. EDT]; 9/11 Commission, "[MFR] of the Interview of Kevin J. Nasypany of the NEADS Conducted by Team 8, 01/22/2004" [interview continued on 01/23/2004], RG 148: Records of Commissions of the Legislative Branch, 1928–2007, NARA, Washington, D.C.

172. This was probably Canadian naval officer Capt. Mike Jellinek, second in command to Maj. Gen. Eric A. Findley, Canadian Forces, the CMOC battle staff director and NORAD director of operations.

173. 9/11 Commission, second public hearing: transcript, panel 1, day 2 [May 23, 2003], unsworn testimony of Maj Gen Larry Arnold, USAF (Ret); 9/11 Commission, MFR, Arnold, 02/03/2004; Filson, *Air War Over America*, p 56; 9/11 Commission, "[MFR] of NORAD Field Site Visit and Interview with Rick Findley of Canadian Forces Conducted by Team 8, 03/01/2004," RG 148: Records of Commissions of the Legislative Branch, 1928–2007, Center for Legislative Archives, NARA, Washington, D.C. [http://media.nara.gov/9-11/MFR/t-0148-911MFR-00789.pdf, accessed Nov 18, 2009]; "Embassy Row: Deter, detect, defend," *Washington Times*, May 9, 2008. [http://www.washingtontimes.com/news/2008/may/09/embassy-row-16680850//print/, accessed Nov 20, 2009.]

174. "9/11: The World Remembers," CNN American Morning, transcript of interview by Jonathan Freed, CNN correspondent, of now Lt Gen Rick Findley, NORAD deputy commander, aired Sep 11, 2006, 6:00 E[D]T. [http://transcripts.cnn.com/TRANSCRIPTS/0609/11/ltm.02.html, accessed Nov 20, 2009.]

175. Excerpt, "9/12, 2001," from Desmond Morton, *A Military History of Canada*, Random House, Inc., 2009 [http://www.randomhouse.com/catalog/display.pperl?isbn=9781551991405&view=excerpt, accessed Nov 20, 2009]; William B. Scott, "Exercise Jump-Starts Response to Attacks," *Aviation Week & Space Technology*, Jun 3, 2002; Scott Simmie, "'Northern Guardian': The Scene at NORAD on Sept. 11," *Toronto Star*, Dec 9, 2001. [http://www.oilempire.us/norad.html, accessed Nov 20, 2009.]

176. Bronner, "9/11 Live: The NORAD Tapes," Aug 2006, NEADS audio tape, 8:52:40 a.m. [EDT]; "Transcripts from Voice Recorder," 11 Sep 2001, 1227Z-1417Z, NEADS, DRM 2, Dat 2, Channel 2 MCC-OP, 12:53:16–12:54:04 [8:53:16–8:54:04 a.m. EDT] and 12:54:57–12:55:58 [8:54:57–8:55:58 a.m. EDT].

177. Miles Kara, e-mails to P. D. Jones, Jun 6, 2011, 5:36 p.m. and 10:19 p.m. EDT; and Jun 7, 2011, 1:20 p.m. EDT. DOT, FAA, MacDonald, Cape TRACON, Memorandum, subj: Information: Partial Transcript; Presidential 9/11 Commission Inquiry; from Manager, Cape TRACON, K90-1, to Pres-

idential 9/11 Commission, Oct 10, 2003, attaching transcript covering the Cape TRACON HIGH Arrival position from 1247–1259 UTC, Sep 11, 2001: see 12:50:59 [8:50:59 a.m. EDT] [http://aal77.com/faa/faa_atc/otis/5%20K90%206%20PARTIAL%20TRANSCRIPTS%203%20POSITIONS%20FLIGHT%20DATA,%20SUPERVISORS%20CONSOLE,%20HIGH%20AR.PDF, accessed Nov 4, 2004]; "Transcripts from Voice Recorder," 11 Sep 2001, 1227Z–1417Z, NEADS, DRM 2, Dat 2, Channel 15 [AST], TSgt Jeffrey Richmond at 12:57:55 [8:57:55 a.m. EDT]; *The 9/11 Commission Final Report*, p 20; "Otis Scramble, Take Off, Lacking a Mission, 0852–0903 EDT," slide 2, prepared by 9/11 Commission Team 8 staff member Miles Kara, n.d. [http://www.scribd.com/doc/13723849/T8-B16-Otis-Lang ley-and-AF1-Fdr-2-of-2-Radar-Maps-Otis-Scrambles-129, accessed May 27, 2009.]

178. *The 9/11 Commission Final Report*, p 20 and p 459, endnote 119.

179. Direct quote from Kevin Dennehy, "'I thought it was the start of World War III,'" *Cape Cod Times*, Aug 21, 2002. [http://archive.capecodonline.com/special/terror/ithought21.htm, accessed Dec 8, 2009.]

180. Direct quote from 9/11 Commission, MFR, Roebuck, 09/22/2003, RG 148, NARA, Washington, D.C. Timeline prepared by 9/11 Commission Team 8 staffer Miles Kara, "Panta 45 and 46 Scramble," entry for 8:46:21, transmission from ZBW 18RA [Boston Center radar associate position]. [http://www.scribd.com/doc/18664568/T8-B21-NEADS-Floor-3-of-3-Fed-Time-Line-Panta-45-and-46-Scramble-289, accessed Dec 8, 2009.]

181. 9/11 Commission, MFR, Fox, 10/29/2003, RG 148, NARA, Washington, D.C

182. "Transcripts from Voice Recorder," 11 Sep 2001, 1227Z–1417Z, NEADS, DRM 2, Dat 2, Channel 2 MCC-OP, 12:57:09–12:59:03 [8:57:09–8:59:03 a.m. EDT], direct quote at 12:57:09 [8:57:09 a.m. EDT].

183. U.S. Department of Transportation, Federal Aviation Administration, Karen L. Goff, Quality Assurance Technician, Boston ARTCC [Air Route Traffic Control Center], Memorandum, subj: Information: Full Transcript Request for the National Commission on Terrorist Attacks Upon the United States [9/11 Commission]; from Boston ARTCC to National Commission on Terrorist Attacks Upon the United States, Oct 7, 2003, attaching transcript covering the Boston ARTCC Cape Sector, Sector 18, Radar Position [name unknown] from 1254–1330 UTC, Sep 11, 2001: see 12:55:22–12:55:38 [8:55:22–8:55:38 a.m. EDT] (Cape Sector-Duffy exchange); 13:01:17 [9:01:17 a.m. EDT] (Duffy to Cape Sector); and 13:01:26 [9:01:26 a.m. EDT] (Cape Sector to Duffy) [http://www.scribd.com/doc/13653219/T8-B20-Miles-Kara-Work-Files-NEADS-Trip-3-of-3-Fdr-Transcript-Boston-ARTCC-Cape-Sector-Sector-18109, accessed Nov 3, 2009]; "Transcripts from Voice Recorder," 11 Sep 2001, 1227Z–1417Z, NEADS, DRM 2, Dat 2, Channel 2 MCC-OP, 12:57:09–12:59:03 [8:57:09–8:59:03 a.m. EDT]; *The 9/11 Commission Final Report*, p 20 and p 459, endnote 120.

184. Bronner, "9/11 Live: The NORAD Tapes," Aug 2006, quote from ID [Identification] Tech[nician] SrA Stacia Rountree at 9:03:17 a.m. EDT. Rountree fielded the phone call from the FAA's New York Center on Long Island. *The 9/11 Commission Final Report*, p 23 and p 460, endnote 134. The 9/11 Commission relied here on FAA and NEADS interviews, rather than on the NEADS operations floor audio files, which are the source for Michael Bronner's *Vanity Fair* article.

185. United Airlines Flight 175 was a Boeing 767-222, according to FAA Registry, Aircraft, N-Number Inquiry Results: N612UA [United Airlines Flight 175]. Don Dillman of American Airlines told 9/11 Commission staffers that United Airlines Flight 175 was, like American Airlines Flight 11, a Boeing 767-200. 9/11 Commission, MFR, Dillman, 11/18/2003, RG 148, NARA, Washington, D.C.

186. *The 9/11 Commission Final Report*, p 7 and p 454, endnotes 40–41, citing United Airlines, FAA, and NTSB reports and documents.

187. Ibid., pp 7, 21.

188. DOT, FAA, "Summary of Air Traffic Hijack Events, September 11, 2001," Timelines: American Airlines Flight 11 and United Airlines Flight 175, The National Security Archive, The September 11th Sourcebooks, NSAEBB No. 165, Doc 7; 9/11 Commission MFRs: Bottiglia, 10/01/2003; Marr, 01/23/2004; and Nasypany, 01/22/2004 [cont'd on 01/23/2004], all RG 148, NARA, Washington, D.C.; *The 9/11 Commission Final Report*, pp 7, 21–22, and 23 and pp 459–60, endnotes 125–130 and 134, citing various FAA and NEADS documents; Farmer, *The Ground Truth*, p 142.

189. *The 9/11 Commission Final Report*, p 22.

190. "Transcripts from Voice Recorder," 11 Sep 2001, 1227Z–1417Z, NEADS, DRM 1, Dat 2, Channel 4 ID1—OP Position, direct quote at 13:03:20 [9:03:20 a.m. EDT]; Bronner, "9/11 Live: The

NORAD Tapes," Aug 2006, NEADS audio tape, 9:03:17 a.m. [EDT].

191. Bronner, "9/11 Live: The NORAD Tapes," Aug 2006, NEADS audio tape, 9:04:50 a.m. [EDT]; "Transcripts from Voice Recorder," 11 Sep 2001, 1227Z-1417Z, NEADS, DRM 2, Dat 2, Channel 2 MCC-OP, 13:08:42 [9:08:42 a.m. EDT].

192. "Transcripts from Voice Recorder," 11 Sep 2001, 1227Z-1417Z, NEADS, DRM 2, Dat 2, Channel 2 MCC-OP, direct quote at 13:04:04 [9:04:04 a.m. EDT]; Bronner, "9/11 Live: The NORAD Tapes," Aug 2006, NEADS audio tape, direct quote at 9:03:52 a.m. [EDT].

193. "Transcripts from Voice Recorder," 11 Sep 2001, 1227Z-1417Z, NEADS, DRM 2, Dat 2, Channel 2 MCC-OP, 13:04:15–13:07:47 [9:04:15–9:07:47 a.m. EDT].

194. Ibid., 13:07:47–13:07:59 and 13:09:00, with direct quote at 13:07:59 [9:07:47–9:07:59 and 9:09:00, with direct quote at 9:07:59 a.m. EDT]. Bronner, "9/11 Live: The NORAD Tapes," Aug 2006, NEADS audio tape, 9:07:20 a.m. [EDT]; *The 9/11 Commission Final Report*, pp 23–24.

195. Direct quote from Bronner, "9/11 Live: The NORAD Tapes," Aug 2006 and "Transcripts from Voice Recorder, 11 September 2001 1227Z-1417Z, Northeast Air Defense Sector, Rome, NY," DRM 2, Dat 2, Channel 2 MCC-OP, 13:08:49–13:08:58 [9:08:49–9:08:58 a.m. EDT]. 9/11 Commission MFRs: Nasypany, 01/22/2004 [cont'd on 01/23/2004], and Marr, 01/23/2004, both RG 148, NARA, Washington, D.C.

196. Direct quote from Bronner, "9/11 Live: The NORAD Tapes," Aug 2006.

197. *The 9/11 Commission Final Report*, p 24 and p 460, endnote 137, citing NEADS audio file and Marr and Arnold interviews.

198. Direct quotes from 9/11 Commission, MFR, Nasypany, 01/22/2004 [cont'd on 01/23/2004], RG 148, NARA, Washington, D.C.

199. "Transcripts from Voice Recorder," 11 Sep 2001, 1227Z-1417Z, NEADS, DRM 2, Dat 2, Channel 69 MCC-OP, 13:10:09–13:11:35 [9:10:09–9:11:35 a.m. EDT].

200. Direct quote from Bronner, "9/11 Live: The NORAD Tapes," Aug 2006.

201. Ibid.

202. *The 9/11 Commission Final Report*, p 24 and p 460, endnotes 138–140, citing 9/11 Commission analysis of FAA radar data and air traffic control transmissions and FAA documents.

203. Ibid., pp 10 and 29.

204. The Panta flight exited the holding pattern at 9:13 a.m. EDT, flew to Manhattan, and reached New York City at 9:25 a.m. EDT. *The 9/11 Commission Final Report*, p 24 and p 460, endnote 136, citing 9/11 Commission staff interviews of Nash and Duffy.

205. Ibid., p 22 and p 460, endnote 130, noting that the 9/11 Commission "determined that the impact time was 9:03:11 based on . . . [its] analysis of FAA radar data and air traffic control software logic."

206. In more than five hours flying over New York, Duffy and Nash "escorted about 100 aircraft out of the area before returning to Otis", according to Susan Rosenfeld and Charles J. Gross, *Air National Guard at 60: A History*, Air National Guard, PA07-721, n.d., p 36. Duffy and Nash flew combat patrols over New York for four and a half hours, and Majs Martin Richard and Robert Martyn worked with them and then relieved them, according to Vittner, "[Otis] Historian's Report." Spencer, *Touching History*, p 245; 9/11 Commission MFRs: Duffy, 01/07/2004, and Nash, 10/14/2003, both RG 148, NARA, Washington, D.C.; 9/11 Commission transcript and typed notes of intvw, Filson with Duffy.

207. 9/11 Commission MFRs: Duffy, 01/07/2004, and Nash, 10/14/2003, both RG 148, NARA, Washington, D.C.

208. Direct quote from transcript of intvw, Duffy, Aug 12, 2009, conducted by Johnson, Stewart, and Dysart.

209. "Transcripts from Voice Recorder," 11 Sep 2001, 1227Z–1417Z, NEADS, DRM 2, Dat 2, Channel 15 [AST], 13:20:57 [9:20:57 a.m. EDT]; *The 9/11 Commission Final Report*, p 26 and p 461, endnote 148, citing NEADS audio file, identification technician position, channel 7, 9:21:10 a.m.; Bronner, "9/11 Live: The NORAD Tapes," Aug 2006, NEADS audio tape, 9:21:37 a.m. [EDT].

210. "Transcripts from Voice Recorder," 11 Sep 2001, 1227Z-1417Z, NEADS, DRM 2, Dat 2, Channel 2 MCC-OP, 13:22:05 [9:22:05 a.m. EDT]; *The 9/11 Commission Final Report*, p 26 and p 461, endnote 149, citing NEADS audio file, MCC, channel 2, 9:21:50 a.m. EDT; Bronner, "9/11 Live: The NORAD Tapes," Aug 2006, NEADS audio tape, 9:21:50 a.m. [EDT].

211. Direct quote from 9/11 Commission, MFR, Nasypany, 01/22/2004 [cont'd on 01/23/2004],

RG 148, NARA, Washington, D.C.

212. "Transcripts from Voice Recorder, 11 September 2001 1227Z-1417Z, Northeast Air Defense Sector, Rome, NY," DRM 2, Dat 2, Channel 2 MCC-OP, direct quote at 13:22:05 [9:22:05 a.m. EDT]; Bronner, "9/11 Live: The NORAD Tapes," Aug 2006, direct quote from NEADS audio tape, 9:21:50 a.m. [EDT]. *The 9/11 Commission Final Report*, p 26 and p 461, endnote 149, citing NEADS audio file, MCC, channel 2, 9:21:50 a.m. EDT.

213. One of Nasypany's staffers said that the fighter officer told them to "forget the tail chase." "Transcripts from Voice Recorder," 11 Sep 2001, 1227Z-1417Z, NEADS, DRM 2, Dat 2, Channel 2 MCC-OP, direct quote at 13:25:47 [9:25:47 a.m. EDT] [background voice].

214. Marr later recalled that he was concerned about the "low reliability" of the report from Boston Center, because American Flight 11, said to be heading south, would have been out of Boston Center's radar range. Direct quotes from 9/11 Commission, MFR, Marr, 01/23/2004, RG 148, NARA, Washington, D.C.

215. "Transcripts from Voice Recorder," 11 Sep 2001, 1227Z-1417Z, NEADS, DRM 2, Dat 2, Channel 2 MCC-OP, 13:27:04 [9:27:04 a.m. EDT] [background voice].

216. Bronner, "9/11 Live: The NORAD Tapes," Aug 2006; *The 9/11 Commission Final Report*, p 465, endnote 238, citing Borgstrom. Marr recalled directing the Langley fighters to battle stations, but he did "not recall considering a scramble." Shortly thereafter, he said he scrambled the Langley F–16s to protect Washington, D.C. Direct quote from 9/11 Commission, MFR, Marr, 01/23/2004, RG 148, NARA, Washington, D.C.

217. 9/11 Commission, Langley AFB Site Visit Interviews: MFR of an interview with Craig Borgstrom conducted by Team 8, 12/01/2003 [http://www.scribd.com/doc/19057171/DH-B2-Langley-MFRs-Fdr-12103-MFR-Craig-Borgstrom, accessed Mar 1, 2010], MFR of an interview with Brad Derrig conducted by Team 8, 12/01/2003 [http://www.scribd.com/doc/19057167/DH-B2-Langley-MFRs-Fdr-12103-MFR-Brad-Derrig, accessed Mar 1, 2010], and MFR of an interview with Dean Eckmann conducted by Team 8, 12/01/2003. [http://www.scribd.com/doc/19057174/DH-B2-Langley-MFRs-Fdr-12103-MFR-Dean-Eckmann, accessed Mar 1, 2010]; Spencer, *Touching History*, pp 118 and 148; Filson, *Air War Over America*, p 63.

218. "Transcripts from Voice Recorder," 11 Sep 2001, 1227Z–1417Z, NEADS, DRM 2, Dat 2, Channel 2 MCC-OP. Nasypany told Maj James Fox to "scramble Langley, head them towards the Washington area[.]" [direct quote at 13:22:47 (9:22:47 a.m. EDT)]; other information at 13:24:20 (9:24:20 a.m. EDT), 13:24:23 (9:24:23 a.m. EDT), and 13:30:41 (9:30:41 a.m. EDT). 9/11 Commission MFRs: Nasypany, 01/22/2004 [cont'd on 01/23/2004], and Borgstrom, 12/01/2003; both RG 148, NARA, Washington, D.C.; *The 9/11 Commission Final Report*, p 27.

219. Direct quote from 9/11 Commission, MFR, Borgstrom, 12/01/2003.

220. 9/11 Commission, MFR, Eckmann, 12/01/2003.

221. Marr told 9/11 Commission staffers that Langley fighters were routinely scrambled to Warning Area [Whiskey] 306. 9/11 Commission, MFR, Watson, et al., 10/27/2003 [Marr's initial briefing to 9/11 Commission staff], RG 148, NARA, Washington, D.C. But SSgt William Huckabone, the NEADS weapons technician handling the Langley fighters, clearly referred to "Whiskey *386*" in an exchange with the navy air traffic controller at Giant Killer. Bronner, "9/11 Live: The NORAD Tapes," Aug 2006, direct quote from NEADS audio tape, 9:34:12 a.m. [EDT], italics added.

222. 9/11 Commission: MFR, Nasypany, 01/22/2004 [cont'd on 01/23/2004], RG 148, NARA, Washington, D.C.; Visit to 119th Fighter Wing, Detachment One, Langley AFB, MFR of an interview with Marsh Ljelvik conducted by Team 8, 10/07/2003 [http://www.scribd.com/doc/20954109/Mfr-Nara-t8-Dodusaf-119th-Fighter-Wing-Visit-10703-00677, accessed Mar 1, 2010]; "[MFR] of a Meeting with Langley Tower Personnel [Kevin Griffith and Raymond Halford] of the U.S. Air Force Conducted by Team 8, 10/06/2003," RG 148: Records of Commissions of the Legislative Branch, 1928–2007, Center for Legislative Archives, NARA, Washington, D.C. [http://media.nara.gov/9-11/MFR/t-0148-911MFR-00676.pdf, accessed Mar 8, 2010]; Langley AFB Site Visit interview, MFR of an interview with Dwayne Acoff and with Robert Lugaro conducted by Team 8, 12/01/2003 [http://www.scribd.com/doc/19057175/DH-B2-Langley-MFRs-Fdr-12103-MFR-Dwayne-Acoff-and-Robert-Lugaro, accessed Mar 8, 2010]; "[MFR] of the Norfolk TRACON visit with John Harter, Michael Strother[,] and William Casson of the Federal Aviation Administration Conducted by Team 8, 12/01/2003," RG 148: Records of Commissions of the Legislative Branch, 1928–2007, Center for Legislative Archives, NARA, Washington, D.C. [http://media.nara.gov/9-11/MFR/t-0148-911MFR-00

793.pdf, accessed Mar 8, 2010]; *The 9/11 Commission Final Report*, p 27 and p 461, endnote 153, citing Eckmann interview and FAA transcripts for Quit 25 [Eckmann] and Peninsular Radar and East Feeder Radar positions. [http://www.9-11commission.gov/report/911Report_Ch1.pdf, accessed Aug 20, 2007.]

223. 9/11 Commission MFRs: Eckmann, 12/01/2003, and Ljelvik, 10/07/2003. 9/11 Commission, Langley AFB radar maps for Sep 11, 2001, "Quit 25: Langley Scramble, Peninsula Sector, Norfolk TRACON 0930–0932 EDT," slide prepared by Team 8 staffer Miles Kara, n.d. [http://www.scribd.com/doc/18663367/T8-B16-Otis-Langley-AF-One-1-of-2-Fdr-Slides-Radar-Maps-Langley-Scramble-Order-136?autodown=pdf, accessed Sep 17, 2009.]

224. SSgt William Huckabone was the first NEADS air defender to notice that the Quit flight was off course. Bronner, "9/11 Live: The NORAD Tapes," Aug 2006, NEADS audio tape, 9:34:12 a.m. [EDT]. 9/11 Commission, MFR, Nasypany, 01/22/2004 [cont'd on 01/23/2004], RG 148, NARA, Washington, D.C. *The 9/11 Commission Final Report*, pp 27 and 461, endnote 150, citing NEADS audio file, MCC, Channel 2, 9:22:34 [sic] a.m. EDT. The correct time is indicated in the following: "Transcripts from Voice Recorder, 11 September 2001 1227Z–1417Z, Northeast Air Defense Sector, Rome, NY," DRM 2, Dat 2, Channel 2 MCC-OP, 13:34:19–13:35:01 [9:34:19–9:35:01 a.m. EDT] and confirmed at DRM 2, Dat 2, Channel 3 SD2-TK, 13:34:19–13:35:01 [9:34:19–9:35:01 a.m. EDT]. 9/11 Commission, additional slides for Sep 11, 2001, "Langley Scramble: Takeoff and Approach to Washington[,] D.C." and "Quit 25: Langley Scramble, Washington Center," prepared by Miles Kara, n.d.

225. "Transcripts from Voice Recorder," 11 Sep 2001, 1227Z–1417Z, NEADS, DRM 1, Dat 2, Channel 4 ID1—OP Position, 13:32:23–13:35:25 [9:32:23–9:35:25 a.m. EDT]; DRM 2, Dat 2, Channel 2 MCC-OP, 13:34:23, 13:34:25 [9:34:23, 9:34:25 a.m. EDT] [background voice]. *The 9/11 Commission Final Report*, p 27 and p 461, endnote 151, citing NEADS audio file, ID Tech position, channel 5, 9:32:10 and 9:33:58 a.m. EDT; Bronner, "9/11 Live: The NORAD Tapes," Aug 2006, NEADS audio tape, 9:34:01 a.m. [EDT].

226. Bronner, "9/11 Live: The NORAD Tapes," Aug 2006; *The 9/11 Commission Final Report*, p 27 and p 461, endnotes 151 and 154, citing NEADS audio files and interviews; and 9/11 Commission analysis of FDR, air traffic control, radar, and Pentagon elevation and impact site data.

227. FAA Registry, Aircraft, N-Number Inquiry Results: 644AA [American Airlines Flight 77].

228. *The 9/11 Commission Final Report*, pp 2–4, 8–10 and p 454, endnotes 52 and 53, citing American Airlines report and other documents.

229. Ibid., pp 8–10, 24.

230. Ibid., pp 9–10, 24–25, 27; for the identity of the federal law enforcement agency, see p 9.

231. See endnote 225.

232. The plane was later that morning identified as American Airlines Flight 77. In the weeks after the attacks, radar analysis of its flight revealed that the plane veered away from the White House and headed toward the Pentagon. But NEADS technicians had "no way of knowing this in the moment." Bronner, "9/11 Live: The NORAD Tapes," Aug 2006.

233. Ibid., NEADS audio tape, 9:35:41 a.m. [EDT]. "Transcripts from Voice Recorder," 11 Sep 2001, 1227Z–1417Z, NEADS, DRM 1, Dat 2, Channel 4 ID1—OP Position, 13:36:19–13:36:20 [background voice].

234. Bronner, "9/11 Live: The NORAD Tapes," Aug 2006.

235. Ibid., NEADS audio tape, 9:36:23 a.m. [EDT]. "Transcripts from Voice Recorder," 11 Sep 2001, 1227Z-1417Z, NEADS, DRM 2, Dat 2, Channel 2 MCC-OP, 13:36:37–13:37:38 [9:36:37–9:37:38 a.m. EDT]; HQ NORAD, NORAD Regulation 55–7, 6 Jul 1990, "Operations: Airborne Surveillance of Hijacked Aircraft." [http://www.fas.org/spp/military/docops/norad/reg55007.htm, accessed Mar 16, 2010.]

236. Direct quote from *The 9/11 Commission Final Report*, p 27; p 461, endnote 152. Bronner, "9/11 Live: The NORAD Tapes," Aug 2006, NEADS audio tape, 9:36:23 a.m. [EDT]; "Transcripts from Voice Recorder," 11 Sep 2001, 1227Z-1417Z, NEADS, DRM 2, Dat 2, Channel 2 MCC-OP, 13:36:37–13:37:34 [9:36:37–9:37:34 a.m. EDT]; Farmer, *The Ground Truth*, p 196, text and quotes from MCC transcript, at 9:39:59–9:40:04 a.m. EDT; Spencer, *Touching History*, p 113; HQ NORAD, NORAD Regulation 55–7, 6 Jul 1990. 9/11 Commission MFRs: Fox, 10/29/2003; Nasypany, 01/22/2004 [cont'd on 01/23/2004]; Marr, 01/23/2004, all RG 148, NARA, Washington, D.C.; and "[MFR] of the Interview of Ian Sanderson of the NEADS Conducted by Team 8, 10/29/2003, RG 148: Records

of Commissions of the Legislative Branch, 1928–2007, Center for Legislative Archives, NARA, Washington, D.C. [http://media.nara.gov/9-11/MFR/t-0148-911MFR-00776.pdf, accessed Feb 5, 2009.]

237. Almost exactly an hour after the impact at 1 World Trade Center, Nasypany exhorted his team, "We've got to find that American Airlines [11] . . . he is the key to this whole thing[.]" Transcripts of NEADS tapes prepared by Miles Kara, times approximate: DRM 3, Dat 2, Channel 8, Rm 112, direct quote at 9:46:47 a.m. EDT. [http://www.scribd.com/doc/13723863/T8-B20-Miles-Kara-Work-Files-NEADS-Trip-2-of-3-Fdr-NEADS-CDs, accessed Jul 20, 2009.] The status of American Flight 11 was uncertain after the strike at the Pentagon and just before United Flight 93 crashed. "Transcripts from Voice Recorder," 11 Sep 2001, 1227Z–1417Z, NEADS, DRM 1, Dat 2, Channel 4 ID1—OP Position, 14:02:13 [10:02:13 a.m. EDT].

238. The primary radar track, Bravo 032, of what was later determined to be American Flight 77 faded over Washington, D.C., at 9:38 a.m. EDT. *The 9/11 Commission Final Report*, p 27 and p 461, endnote 154, citing NEADS audio file, MCC, channel 2, 9:38:02; Deskins interview. 9/11 Commission, MFR, Nasypany, 01/22/2004 [cont'd on 01/23/2004], RG 148, NARA, Washington, D.C. "Transcripts from Voice Recorder, 11 September 2001 1227Z-1417Z, Northeast Air Defense Sector, Rome, NY," DRM 2, Dat 2, Channel 2 MCC-OP, 13:37:46–13:37:59 [9:37:46–9:37:59 a.m. EDT]; DRM 2, Dat 2, Channel 15 [AST], 13:36:29–13:38:11 [9:36:29–9:38:11 a.m. EDT]. Transcripts of NEADS tapes prepared by Miles Kara, times approximate: DRM 1, Dat 2, Channel 17 TT [Tracker Tech] OP, 9:33:55–9:38:35 a.m. EDT; DRM 1, Dat 2, Channel 18 TT TK, 9:35–9:40 a.m. EDT; and DRM 3, Dat 2, Channel 8, Rm 112, 9:37:26–9:38:00 a.m. EDT. Bronner, "9/11 Live: The NORAD Tapes," Aug 2006, NEADS audio tape, 9:37:56 a.m. [EDT].

239. Bronner, "9/11 Live: The NORAD Tapes," Aug 2006, NEADS audio tape, 9:37:56 a.m. [EDT].

240. Transcripts of NEADS tapes prepared by Miles Kara, times approximate: DRM 3, Dat 2, Channel 8, Rm 112, 9:38:34 a.m. EDT; *The 9/11 Commission Final Report*, p 27 and p 461, endnote 154.

241. *The 9/11 Commission Final Report*, pp 25–26, 30.

242. Bronner, "9/11 Live: The NORAD Tapes," Aug 2006, direct quote from NEADS audio tape, 9:38:50 a.m. [EDT]. "Transcripts from Voice Recorder," 11 Sep 2001, 1227Z-1417Z, NEADS, DRM 2, Dat 2, Channel 2 MCC-OP, 13:37:46–13:41:45 [9:37:46–9:41:45 a.m. EDT]. *The 9/11 Commission Final Report*, p 27; Transcripts of NEADS tapes prepared by Miles Kara, times approximate: DRM 3, Dat 2, Channel 8, Rm 112, 9:37:26–9:38:00 a.m. EDT, and 9:38:56 a.m. EDT.

243. Direct quote from 9/11 Commission, MFR, Nasypany, 01/22/2004 [cont'd on 01/23/2004], RG 148, NARA, Washington, D.C.

244. "Transcripts from Voice Recorder," 11 Sep 2001, 1227Z-1417Z, NEADS, DRM 2, Dat 2, Channel 3 SD2-TK, 13:36:35–14:04:44 [9:36:35–10:04:44 a.m. EDT]; DRM 2, Dat 2, Channel 15 [AST], 13:37:25, 13:39:17, and 13:39:19 [9:37:25, 9:39:17, and 9:39:19 a.m. EDT]. Bronner, "9/11 Live: The NORAD Tapes," Aug 2006, NEADS audio tape, 9:36:23 a.m. [EDT].

245. Nasypany told 9/11 Commission staffers that the first notice NEADS received came from a CNN report "at approximately 9:48 a.m." Direct quote from 9/11 Commission, MFR, Nasypany, 01/22/2004 [cont'd on 01/23/2004], RG 148, NARA, Washington, D.C. Transcripts of NEADS audio files indicate that NEADS personnel became aware of the Pentagon strike at approximately 9:49 a.m. EDT. "Transcripts from Voice Recorder," 11 Sep 2001, 1227Z–1417Z, NEADS, DRM 2, Dat 2, Channel 15 [AST], 13:49:11 [9:49:11 a.m. EDT]; DRM 2, Dat 2, Channel 2 MCC-OP, 13:50:59 [9:50:59 a.m. EDT]. Transcripts of NEADS tapes prepared by Miles Kara, times approximate: DRM 3, Dat 2, Channel 8, Rm 112, 9:49 a.m. EDT. Alfred Goldberg, Sarandis Papadopoulos, Diane Putney, Nancy Berlage, and Rebecca Welch, *Pentagon 9/11*, Defense Studies Series (Washington, D.C.: Historical Office, Office of the Secretary of Defense, 2007), pp 16–17.

246. Direct quote from *The 9/11 Commission Final Report*, p 38; p 463, endnote 200, citing DOD transcript, Air Threat Conference Call, Sep 11, 2001.

247. "Transcripts from Voice Recorder," 11 Sep 2001, 1227Z-1417Z, NEADS, DRM 2, Dat 2, Channel 2 MCC-OP, direct quote at 13:51:37 and at 13:51:55 [9:51:37 and 9:51:55 a.m. EDT].

248. *The 9/11 Commission Final Report*, p 465, endnote 238. Undated slide prepared by Miles Kara, "Langley Scramble: Proceeds to CAP Point." [http://www.scribd.com/doc/18663367/T8-B16-Otis-Langley-AF-One-1-of-2-Fdr-Slides-Radar-Maps-Langley-Scramble-Order-136?autodown=pdf, accessed Sep 17, 2009.]

249. "Transcripts from Voice Recorder," 11 Sep 2001, 1227Z-1417Z, NEADS, DRM 2, Dat 2, Channel 3 SD2-TK, 13:36:35–14:04:44, direct quote at 14:04:44 [9:36:35–10:04:44 a.m. EDT].

250. "Scene of utter destruction," *Pittsburgh Tribune-Review*, Sep 12, 2001.

251. *The 9/11 Commission Final Report*, pp 30 and 31, and p 462, endnotes 171, 173, and 174, citing NEADS audio files and log book.

252. FAA Registry, Aircraft, N-Number Inquiry Results: 591UA [United Airlines Flight 93].

253. *The 9/11 Commission Final Report*, pp 4, 10; James M. Klatell, "Flight 93 Controller Looks Back," CBS News, Sep 10, 2006. [http://www.cbsnews.com/stories/2006/09/10/september11/main1992 171.shtml, accessed Apr 14, 2011.]

254. *The 9/11 Commission Final Report*, p 11 (quoting United Flight 93 pilot or first officer), p 28 and p 456, endnote 71, citing NTSB, FBI, and FAA reports on cockpit voice recorder [CVR] and FDR. Klatell, "Flight 93 Controller Looks Back," Sep 10, 2006.

255. *The 9/11 Commission Final Report*, p 28 (quote) and p 461, endnote 160, citing FAA memo.

256. Ibid., p 28.

257. Ibid., pp 29, 30.

258. Ibid., p 29 (quote) and p 461, endnote 163, citing FAA memos and audio file. Klatell, "Flight 93 Controller Looks Back," Sep 10, 2006.

259. The passenger revolt aboard United Flight 93 began at 9:57 a.m. EDT. *The 9/11 Commission Final Report*, p 13 and p 457, endnote 85, citing FBI documents, and data from Flight 93 FDR and CVR.

260. *The 9/11 Commission Final Report*, p 30. The impact time for United Flight 93 is supported by FAA and NTSB documents and by 9/11Commission staff analyses of radar, FDR, CVR, air traffic control communications, and other data.

261. The FAA military liaison at Cleveland ARTCC told a NEADS ID technician at approximately 10:07 a.m. EDT that Flight 93 had a bomb on board. "Transcripts from Voice Recorder," 11 Sep 2001, 1227Z–1417Z, NEADS, DRM 1, Dat 2, Channel 4 ID1—OP Position, 14:06:38 [10:06:38 a.m. EDT]; Bronner, "9/11 Live: The NORAD Tapes," Aug 2006, NEADS audio tape, 10:07:16 a.m. [EDT]; *The 9/11 Commission Final Report*, p 30 and p 462, endnote 171, citing NEADS audio file, ID Tech, channel 5, 10:07 a.m.

262. Bronner, "9/11 Live: The NORAD Tapes," Aug 2006, NEADS audio tape, 9:40:57 a.m. [EDT]; Farmer, *The Ground Truth*, pp 194–95, quoting ID Tech transcript (Rountree), at 9:39:33–9:40:29 a.m. EDT.

263. [U.S. Department of Transportation,] Research and Innovative Technology Administration, Bureau of Transportation Statistics, Detailed Statistics: Departures. [http://www.bts.gov/xml/ontimesummarystatistics/src/dstat/OntimeSummaryDepatures[sic]Data.xml, accessed Sep 14, 2009. "Transcripts from Voice Recorder,"11 Sep 2001, 1227Z–1417Z, NEADS, DRM 1, Dat 2, Channel 4 ID1—OP Position, 13:41:11 [9:41:11 a.m. EDT]; 9/11 Commission, "[MFR] of the Interview of HUNTRESS Personnel of the Department of Defense [NEADS] Conducted by Team 8, 01/27/2003," RG 148: Records of Commissions of the Legislative Branch, 1928–2007, Center for Legislative Archives, NARA, Washington, D.C. [http://media.nara.gov/9-11/MFR/t-0148-911MFR-00765.pdf, accessed Feb 2, 2009]; Farmer, *The Ground Truth*, pp 194–95; Spencer, *Touching History*, p 127.

264. Bronner, "9/11 Live: The NORAD Tapes," Aug 2006, NEADS audio tape, 9:40:57 a.m. [EDT]; 9/11 Commission, MFR, McCain, 10/28/2003 [information from intvw cont'd on 01/20/2004], RG 148, NARA, Washington, D.C.; *The 9/11 Commission Final Report*, pp 27–28 and p 461, endnotes 155 and 156, citing Cooper interview; and NEADS audio files, ID Tech position, recorder 1, channel 7, 9:41 a.m. [EDT] and MCC position, channel 2, 9:42:08 a.m. [EDT]; "Transcripts from Voice Recorder," 11 Sep 2001, 1227Z–1417Z, NEADS, DRM 1, Dat 2, Channel 4 ID1—OP Position, 13:41:08–13:45:57 [9:41:08–9:45:57 a.m. EDT]; DRM 2, Dat 2, Channel 15 [AST], 13:41:20–13:48:46 [9:41:20–9:48:46 a.m. EDT].

265. As noted earlier in the text, the NEADS air defenders also established—but did not "forward tell" to NORAD—a track, Bravo 032, on the unidentified aircraft moving away from the White House, later determined to be American Flight 77. 9/11 Commission Team 8 staffer Miles Kara noted: "To 'forward tell' is to link a known track to a specific radar in such a manner that the track can be seen by NORAD echelons above NEADS . . . The Air Threat Conference Call is conclusive concerning what was forward told. When asked for an update NORAD informed the Conference at 9:44 [a.m.

EDT] that the only other hijacked plane it knew about was Delta 1989. There was no mention of United 93 or any other aircraft." Miles Kara, "9-11: Delta 1989," article on his 9-11 Revisited website, n.d. [http://www.orediffer61.org/?cat=18, accessed Mar 26, 2010.] NEADS checklists for the following job titles: mission crew commander/technician [MCC/T Checklist #5, Subj: Hijacked Aircraft, Jul 16, 2001]; air surveillance officer/technician [Checklist #1, Subj: Aircraft Emergency/Hijack/Deviation Procedures, Jul 26, 2001]; senior director/technician [SD/SDT Checklist #6, Subj: Hijacked Checklist, Oct 4, 1997]; tracking technician [Checklist #1, Subj: High Interest Tracks, Jul 30, 2001; and Checklist #2, Subj: Special Interest Tracks, Jul 30, 2001]. [http://www.scribd.com/doc/14141988/NYC-Box-2-NEADS-Transcript-Rome-NY-Fdr-Checklist-NEADS-Response-to-Aircraft-Emergency-Hijack495, accessed Oct 22, 2009]; 9/11 Commission MFRs: HUNTRESS Personnel, 01/27/2003, and McCain, 10/28/2003 [information from intvw cont'd on 01/20/2004]; both RG 148, NARA, Washington, D.C.

266. To facilitate NORAD tracking, it was critical that the victimized aircraft's transponder transmit, or "squawk," Mode 3/A, code 7500, the recognized hijack code. FAA order, "Special Military Operations," Order 7610.4J, effective Nov 3, 1998, Ch. 7. Escort of Hijacked Aircraft, § 4. Forwarding Information, Para. 7-4-2. Position Reports Within NORAD Radar Coverage. [http://web.archive.org/web/20030727162758/www2.faa.gov/ATpubs/MIL/Ch7/mil0704.html, accessed Apr 1, 2009.]

267. Syracuse had reportedly cancelled all of its flying for the morning; Duluth was engaged in night-flying missions, and so there was no one available. "Transcripts from Voice Recorder," 11 Sep 2001, 1227Z-1417Z, NEADS, DRM 2, Dat 2, Channel 2 MCC-OP, 13:42:16–13:47:57 [9:42:16–9:47:57 a.m. EDT]; DRM 2, Dat 2, Channel 15 [AST], 13:50:56–13:51:14 [9:50:56–9:51:14 a.m. EDT]. Farmer, *The Ground Truth*, pp 200–202; Bronner, "9/11 Live: The NORAD Tapes," Aug 2006, especially NEADS audio tape, 9:54:54 a.m. [EDT] regarding the offer of assistance from the Selfridge flight officer; Filson, *Air War Over America*, p 75, citing wing records as to departure time.

268. "Transcripts from Voice Recorder," 11 Sep 2001, 1227Z-1417Z, NEADS, DRM 2, Dat 2, Channel 2 MCC-OP, 13:52:24–13:59:28 [9:52:24–9:59:28 a.m. EDT.

269. "Transcripts from Voice Recorder," 11 Sep 2001, 1227Z-1417Z, NEADS, DRM 2, Dat 2, Channel 2 MCC-OP, 13:59:41–14:01:43 [9:59:41–10:01:43 a.m. EDT] (Selfridge, Toledo, Fargo, and Alpena) and 14:04:14 [10:04:14 a.m. EDT] (Atlantic City). The two fighters from Alpena expected to be in the air at 10:15 a.m. EDT. "Transcripts from Voice Recorder," DRM 2, Dat 2, Channel 2 MCC-OP, 14:05:32–14:05:43 [10:05:32–10:05:43 a.m. EDT]. Penny Carroll, "Selfridge, not Hollywood: A look back at 9-11," *The Wolverine Guard*, Fall 2006. [http://www.michigan.gov/documents/dmva/Fall_06_179624_7.pdf, accessed Sep 17, 2009.]

270. "Transcripts from Voice Recorder," 11 Sep 2001, 1227Z-1417Z, NEADS, DRM 2, Dat 2, Channel 2 MCC-OP, 14:06:10–14:06:16 [10:06:10–10:06:16 a.m. EDT].

271. The response of the battle cab was not recorded, but it is clear that leadership there did not pass shoot-down authority to Nasypany. Ibid., DRM 2, Dat 2, Channel 2 MCC-OP, 13:59:41–14:00:10 [9:59:41–10:00:10 a.m. EDT], with direct quotes at 14:00:13 and 14:00:22 [10:00:13 and 10:00:22 a.m. EDT].

272. Ibid., DRM 1, Dat 2, Channel 4 ID1—OP Position, 13:58:01–14:00:09 [9:58:01–10:00:09 a.m. EDT], direct quote at 13:59:39 [9:59:39 a.m. EDT]. Delta Flight 1989 diverted to Cleveland Airport at 10:05 a.m. EDT and landed there at 10:18 a.m. EDT. U.S. Department of Transportation, Federal Aviation Administration, "Daily Record of Facility Operation," FAA Form 7230-4 (1-94), Date: 9/11/2001, Location: Oberlin, Ohio, Identification: ZOB, Type Facility: ARTCC, Operating Position: Watch Supervisor, Air Traffic Manager: Richard Kettell. [http://www.scribd.com/doc/14353833/T8-B15-Hijacked-Airplaner-2-of-3-Fdr-UA-93-DOT-FAA-Report-of-Aircraft-Accident-and-Daily-Record-of-Facility-Operation, accessed Jul 23, 2009.]

273. "Transcripts from Voice Recorder," 11 Sep 2001, 1227Z-1417Z, NEADS, DRM 2, Dat 2, Channel 2 MCC-OP, 14:01:53–14:01:58, 14:02:22–14:02:46, 14:05:43–14:05:57 [10:01:53–10:01:58, 10:02:22–10:02:46, 10:05:43–10:05:57 a.m. EDT]; DRM 1, Dat 2, Channel 4 ID1—OP Position, 14:03:41–14:05:32 [10:03:41–10:05:32 a.m. EDT]. Bronner, "9/11 Live: The NORAD Tapes," Aug 2006.

274. "Transcripts from Voice Recorder," 11 Sep 2001, 1227Z-1417Z, NEADS, DRM 2, Dat 2, Channel 2 MCC-OP, 14:05:43–14:05:57 [10:05:43–10:05:57 a.m. EDT]; Spencer, *Touching History*, p 223.

275. "Transcripts from Voice Recorder," 11 Sep 2001, 1227Z-1417Z, NEADS, DRM 1, Dat 2,

Channel 4 ID1—OP Position, 14:06:28–14:10:53 [10:06:28–10:10:53 a.m. EDT]; *The 9/11 Commission Final Report*, p 30; Bronner, "9/11 Live: The NORAD Tapes," Aug 2006, NEADS audio tape, 10:07:16 a.m. [EDT].

276. United Flight 93 was presumed to be over or in the vicinity of York, Pennsylvania, and Delta Flight 1989's Mode 3 had just faded over Cleveland. The United flight had, in fact, crashed; the Delta flight had landed safely at Cleveland Airport and was not, as Nasypany thought, heading back east after turning around near Cleveland. "Transcripts from Voice Recorder," 11 Sep 2001, 1227Z–1417Z, NEADS, DRM 2, Dat 2, Channel 2 MCC-OP, 14:12:03–14:14:12 [10:12:03–10:14:12 a.m. EDT].

277. Ibid., DRM 1, Dat 2, Channel 4 ID1—OP Position, 14:14:09–14:15:23 [10:14:09–10:15:23 a.m. EDT]; DRM 2, Dat 2, Channel 2 MCC-OP, 14:14:29–14:15:50 [10:14:29–10:15:50 a.m. EDT]. Bronner, "9/11 Live: The NORAD Tapes," Aug 2006, NEADS audio tape, 10:15:00 a.m. [EDT].

278. Michael D. Sallah and Joe Mahr, "Toledo's Air Guard called to defend U.S. on Sept. 11," Toledo Blade, toledoblade.com, Dec 9, 2001. [http://www.toledoblade.com/apps/pbcs.dll/article?Date=20011209&Category=NEWS28&ArtNo=112090036&Ref=AR, accessed Jan 6, 2009.

279. "Transcripts from Voice Recorder, 11 September 2001 1227Z-1417Z, Northeast Air Defense Sector, Rome, NY," DRM 2, Dat 2, Channel 69 MCC-OP, 13:09:00–13:09:10 [9:09:00–9:09:10 a.m. EDT].

280. Ibid., DRM 2, Dat 2, Channel 2 MCC-OP, 13:58:24–13:58:53 [9:58:24–9:58:53 a.m. EDT]; Filson, *Air War Over America*, pp 71, 73.

281. This according to Maj Martin Richard, presumably. Vittner, "[Otis] Historian's Report." Filson, *Air War Over America*, p 50; Spencer, *Touching History*, p 244. By 9:20 a.m. EDT, NEADS surveillance personnel knew that the additional fighters had been recalled. "Transcripts from Voice Recorder," 11 Sep 2001, 1227Z–1417Z, NEADS, DRM 2, Dat 2, Channel 15 [AST], 13:20:30 [9:20:30 a.m. EDT].

282. Vittner, "[Otis] Historian's Report," directly quoting Maj Martin Richard. Spencer, *Touching History*, pp 243–47; 9/11 Commission, MFR, Duffy, RG 148, NARA, Washington, D.C.

283. Rosenfeld and Gross, *Air National Guard at 60*, p 38.

284. *The 9/11 Commission Final Report*, pp 27, 38, and 40; p 463, endnote 201, citing DOD transcript, Air Threat Conference Call, Sep 11, 2001; p 464, endnote 213, citing 9/11 Commission staff's meeting with President Bush and Vice President Cheney (Apr 29, 2004).

285. Ibid., p 44 (direct quote); p 465, endnotes 235 and 236, citing David Wherley interview (Feb 27, 2004) and USSS memo, Beauchamp to AD-Inspection, September 11 experience, Feb 23, 2004; for information about the federal law enforcement agency, see p 465, endnote 236.

286. Central Intelligence Agency, Director of Central Intelligence George J. Tenet's Testimony Before the Joint Inquiry into Terrorist Attacks Against the United States, unclassified version, Jun 18, 2002. [https://www.cia.gov/news-information/speeches-testimony/2002/dci_testimony_06182002.html, accessed Mar 2, 2011]; "Official: 15 of 19 Sept. 11 hijackers were Saudi," Associated Press, *USA Today*, Feb 6, 2002, updated 06:29 a.m. ET [http://www.usatoday.com/news/world/2002/02/06/saudi. htm, accessed Mar 2, 2011.] Al-Qaeda operatives commonly referred to suicide attacks as "martyrdom operations." Daniel Benjamin and Steven Simon, T*he Age of Sacred Terror: Radical Islam's War Against America* (New York: Random House Trade Paperbacks, 2003), p 28.

287. Eggen and Loeb, "U.S. Intelligence Points To Bin Laden Network," *Washington Post*, Sep 12, 2001, p A1; United Kingdom, Her Majesty's Government, Official Site of the Prime Minister's Office, September 11 attacks—Culpability document, *Responsibility for the Terrorist Atrocities in the United States, 11 September 2001—An Updated Account*, May 15, 2003, pp 2, 3 [http://webarchive.nationalarchives.gov.uk/+/number10.gov.uk/archive/2003/05/september-11-attacks-culpability-document-3682, accessed Mar 7, 2011.]

288. U.S. Department of Defense, American Forces Press Service, National Guard Bureau, "The Operation Desert Shield/Desert Storm Timeline," Aug 8, 2000. From the 1991 "Defense Almanac" [http://www.defense.gov/news/newsarticle.aspx?id= 45404, accessed Jan 24, 2011]; Wright, *The Looming Tower*, p 270; Tom Cooper, with Brig Gen Ahmad Sadik (IrAF), "Iraqi Invasion of Kuwait, 1990," Sep 16, 2003, 03:02, Air Combat Information Group, Arabian Peninsula & Persian Gulf Database [http://www.acig.org/artman/publish/article_213.shtml, accessed Mar 16, 2011]; Fred Kaplan, "US Forces Arrive in Saudi Arabia," *Boston Globe*, Aug 9, 1990 [http://www.highbeam.com/doc/1P2-8186448.html, accessed Mar 16, 2011.]

289. Wright, *The Looming Tower*, pp 158, 159; Benjamin and Simon, *The Age of Sacred Terror*, pp 105–107; *The 9/11 Commission Final Report*, p 57; Randall D. Law, *Terrorism: A History* (Cambridge, UK/Malden, Mass.: Polity Press, 2009), p 299.

290. The date of the World Trade Center bombing, Feb 26, 1993, was the second anniversary of Kuwait's liberation by U.S. and coalition forces following its invasion by Saddam Hussein. Phil Hirschkorn, "Top Terrorist Convictions Upheld," CNN.com, Apr 4, 2003, posted 2335 GMT [http://edition.cnn.com/2003/LAW/04/04/terrorism.yousef/, accessed May 18, 2011.]

291. Wright, *The Looming Tower*, pp 188–89, 202, 204–205, 235–36, 246, 255–58; Law, *Terrorism*, pp 302–303, 304; *The 9/11 Commission Final Report*, pp 60, 67; Benjamin and Simon, *The Age of Sacred Terror*, p 224. Memorandum for Air Force Chief of Staff and Secretary of the Air Force from 12AF/CC James F. Record, Lt Gen, USAF, Oct 31, 1996, attaching Lt Gen James F. Record, "Independent Review of the Khobar Towers Bombing," [http://www.au.af.mil/au/awc/awcgate/khobar/recordf.htm, accessed Apr 5, 2011]; John L. Esposito, *Islam: The Straight Path* (New York/Oxford: Oxford University Press, 2005), p 262.

292. *The 9/11 Commission Final Report*, p 67.

293. Osama bin Laden, "Declaration of War against the Americans Occupying the Land of the Two Holy Places," Aug 23, 1996 [http://www.mideastweb.org/osamabinladen1.htm, accessed Jan 14, 2011.]

294. "Text of Fatwa Urging Jihad Against Americans—1998," *Al-Quds al-Arabi*, London, Feb 23, 1998, translation from the Arabic under the headline "Text of World Islamic Front's Statement Urging Jihad Against Jews and Crusaders" [http://www.mideastweb.org/osamabinladen2.htm, accessed Jan 14, 2011.]

295. Tenet's Testimony Before the Joint Inquiry into Terrorist Attacks Against the United States, unclassified version, Jun 18, 2002; Wright, *The Looming Tower*, pp 270–72, 297–98, 299–300, 319–20; Phil Hirschkorn, "Four Embassy Bombers Get Life," CNN.com, Oct 21, 2001, posted 10:58 a.m. EDT (1458 GMT) [http://edition.cnn.com/2001/LAW/10/19/embassy.bombings/, accessed May 18, 2011]; Esposito, *Islam: The Straight Path*, p 262.

296. Benjamin and Simon, *The Age of Sacred Terror*, p 156, citing Osama bin Laden videotape released Dec 27, 2001, accessed by the authors at www.fas.org/irp/world/para/ladin_122701.pdf.

297. Ibid., pp 156–57.

298. Ibid., p 157, directly quoting Osama bin Laden interview with Tayseer Alouni, Afghanistan, al-Jazeera, Oct 2001; translation accessed by the authors at www.cnn.com/2002/WORLD/asiapcf/south/02/05/binladen.transcript/.

299. Ibid., pp 156–61.

300. Direct quote from The White House, President George W. Bush, Office of the Press Secretary, Address to a Joint Session of Congress and the American People, United States Capitol, Washington, D.C., Sep 20, 2001, 9:00 p.m. EDT. [http://www.whitehouse.gov/news/releases/2001/09/print/20010920-8.html, accessed Jun 12, 2008]; Peter Ford, "Why Do They Hate Us?" *Christian Science Monitor*, Sep 27, 2001 [http://www.csmonitor.com/2001/0927/p1s1-wogi.html, accessed Feb 11, 2011.]

301. *The 9/11 Commission Final Report*, p 2; Kenneth Katzman, *Terrorism: Near Eastern Groups and State Sponsors*, 2001, Congressional Research Service (CRS), The Library of Congress, report no. RL31119, Sep 10, 2001 (later revised, Feb 13, 2002), p CRS-2. [http://www.mipt.org/pdf/crs_r/311 19.pdf, accessed Jan 8, 2008]; David Zeidan, "The Islamic Fundamentalist View of Life as a Perennial Battle," *Middle East Review of International Affairs* [MERIA] *Journal*, vol 5, no 4 (Dec 2001) [http://meria.idc.ac.il/journal/2001/issue4/jv5n4a2.htm, accessed Feb 4, 2011.]

302. Benjamin and Simon, *The Age of Sacred Terror*, p 220.

303. U.S. Congress Joint Inquiry into Intelligence Community Activities before and after the Terrorist Attacks of September 11, 2001, *Joint inquiry into intelligence community activities before and after the terrorist attacks of September 11, 2001: report of the U.S. Senate Select Committee on Intelligence and U.S. House Permanent Select Committee on Intelligence together with additional views* Filed Dec 20, 2002; S. Rept. 107–351 and H. Rept. 107–792, 107th Congress, 2d Session. Washington, D.C.: U.S. Government Printing Office, 2002 [http://purl.access.gpo.gov/GPO/LPS34039, accessed Nov 20, 2007] Part 2: Narrative—The Attacks of September 11, 2001, p 193. [http://www.gpoaccess.gov/serialset/creports/pdf/part2.pdf, accessed Jun 16, 2008.]

304. Ibid., p 193, quoting Jenkins and Woolsey.

305. Ibid., p 193. Benjamin and Simon, *The Age of Sacred Terror*, p 221; Law, *Terrorism*, p 278.

306. In May 1993, the FBI learned "from a foreign source" that bin Laden was providing financial backing for Rahman's efforts at jihad and, specifically, for the Islamist cell involved in a plot to attack New York City landmarks. Wright, *The Looming Tower*, pp 3, 177, 181–82, quote on p 3; On Oct 8, 2002, a report by Eleanor Hill, staff director of the Joint Inquiry Staff assisting the Senate Select Committee on Intelligence and the House Permanent Select Committee on Intelligence in their inquiry into the 9/11 attacks, revealed that bin Laden had helped pay for Nosair's legal defense. U.S. Congress Joint Inquiry into Intelligence Community Activities before and after the Terrorist Attacks of September 11, 2001, Joint Inquiry Staff Statement, Part I, Eleanor Hill, Staff Director, Joint Inquiry Staff, Sep 18, 2002 [http://i.cnn.net/cnn/2002/ALLPOLITICS/09/18/intelligence.hearings/intel.911. report.pdf,a ccessed Sep 19, 2007]; Greg B. Smith, "Bin Laden Bankrolled Kahane Killer Defense," *New York Daily News*, Oct 9, 2002, 8:06 a.m. [http://www.nydailynews.com/archives /news/2002/10/09 /2002-10-09_bin_laden_ bankrolled_kahane_.html, accessed Mar 8, 2011]; Benjamin and Simon, *The Age of Sacred Terror*, pp 4–5.

307. Benjamin and Simon, *The Age of Sacred Terror*, p 6.

308. Ibid., pp 7–14. Wright, *The Looming Tower*, pp 176–79, 236; *The 9/11 Commission Final Report*, pp 71–72; Law, *Terrorism*, pp 301–302.

309. Wright, *The Looming Tower*, pp 176–79; Benjamin and Simon, *The Age of Sacred Terror*, pp 15–19; *The 9/11 Commission Final Report*, pp 71–72; Law, *Terrorism*, p 302.

310. Wright, *The Looming Tower*, pp 235–36; Benjamin and Simon, *The Age of Sacred Terror*, pp 20–25, 449; *The 9/11 Commission Final Report*, pp 73, 147; U.S. Congress Joint Inquiry, *Report*, Dec 20, 2002, p 192.

311. Wright, *The Looming Tower*, pp 235–36; Benjamin and Simon, *The Age of Sacred Terror*, pp 20–25; *The 9/11 Commission Final Report*, p 73; U.S. Congress Joint Inquiry, *Report*, Dec 20, 2002, p 192; Brendan Lyons, "Terrorist Foretold 9/11 Towers Plot," *Albany Times-Union*, Sep 22, 2002 [http://www.highbeam.com/doc/1G1-157545047.html, accessed Apr 11, 2011]; "Western Intel Knew bin Laden's Plan Since 1995—German Paper," Agence France-Press, Dec 8, 2001 [http://s3.amazon-aws.com/911timeline/2001/afp120801.html, accessed Apr 11, 2011.]

312. Matthew Brzezinski, "Bust and Boom," *Washington Post*, Dec 30, 2001 [http://propagan-damatrix.com/bust_and_boom.html; http://www.washingtonpost.com/ac2/wp-dyn?pagename=arti-cle&node=&contentId=A14725-2001Dec21, accessed Apr 11, 2011]; Jim Gomez and John Solomon, "Authorities Warned of Hijack Risks," Associated Press, Mar 5, 2002 [http://www.seacoastonline.com/ articles/20020305-NEWS-303059981?cid=sitesearch, accessed Apr 10, 2011]; Lyons, "Terrorist Foretold 9/11 Towers Plot," Sep 22, 2002; "Western Intel Knew bin Laden's Plan Since 1995—German Paper," Dec 8, 2001.

313. Wright, *The Looming Tower*, pp 235–36, 307–308; *The 9/11 Commission Final Report*, pp 73, 147, 149, 153–55, 276; Tenet's Testimony Before the Joint Inquiry into Terrorist Attacks, Jun 18, 2002.

314. Benjamin and Simon, *The Age of Sacred Terror*, p 28.

315. Ibid., pp 28–29; Wright, *The Looming Tower*, pp 217–19.

316. U.S. Congress Joint Inquiry, *Report*, p 214; information contained in a draft CIA analysis, "The 11 September Attacks: A Preliminary Assessment," Nov 19, 2001.

317. Jon Swain, "Revealed: Gadaffi's Air Massacre Plot," Times Online, from *The Sunday Times*, Mar 28, 2004. [http://www.timesonline.co.uk/tol/news/world/article1052614. ece?token=null &print =yes&randnum=1245350048856, accessed Jun 18, 2009.]

318. "Kamikaze Jet Hijacking," n.d. [http://www.rotten.com/library/crime/terrorism/terror-tac-tics/kamikaze-jet-hijacking/, accessed Jun 22, 2010]; "Hijackings in History," articles posted by the staff of NewspaperARCHIVE.com, n.d. Articles from *The News*, Feb 23, 1974. [http://www.newspa-perarchive.com/Articles/Hijackings-in-History.aspx, accessed Jun 22, 2010.]

319. Cockpit Voice Recorder Database: 7 April 1994, Fedex 705. [http://www.tailstrike.com/070 494. htm, accessed May 10, 2011]; Matthew L. Wald, "A Nation Challenged: Warnings; Earlier Hijackings Offered Signals That Were Missed," *New York Times*, Oct 3, 2001. [http://www.nytimes.com /2001/ 10/03/us/a-nation-challenged-warnings-earlier-hijackings-offered-signals-that-were-missed. html?pagewanted=print&src=pm, accessed Jan 31, 2001.

320. Wald, "A Nation Challenged," Oct 3, 2001; "Hijackings in History," article from the *Daily Herald*, Sep 13, 1994; "Kamikaze Jet Hijacking," n.d.

321. The Armed Islamic Group was also known as the GIA, Groupe Islamique Armé, or al-Ja-

ma'ah al-Islamiyyah al-Musallaha.

322. *The 9/11 Commission Final Report*, p 345; Wald, "A Nation Challenged," Oct 3, 2001.

323. U.S. Congress Joint Inquiry, *Report*, Dec 20, 2002, p 209; Wald, "A Nation Challenged," Oct 3, 2001; Zachary K. Johnson, "Chronology: The Plots," *Frontline*: "Al Qaeda's New Front," posted Jan 25, 2005 [http://www.pbs.org/wgbh/pages/frontline/shows/front/special/cron.html, accessed Jan 31, 2011]; Lauren Vriens, Council on Foreign Relations *Backgrounder*, "Armed Islamic Group (Algeria, Islamists) (a.k.a. GIA, Groupe Islamique Armé, or al-Jama'ah al-Islamiyyah al-Musallaha)," updated May 27, 2009 [http://www.cfr.org/publication/9154/armed_islamic_group_algeria_islamists.html, accessed Jan 31, 2011]; Thomas Sancton, "Anatomy of a Hijack," *Time*, Jun 24, 2001. [http://www.time.com/time/magazine/article/0,9171,163487,00.html, accessed Jan 31, 2011]; Alan Riding, "The Militant Group Behind the Hijacking," *New York Times*, Dec 27, 1994 [http://query.nytimes.com/gst/fullpage.html?res=9A0DE0D8173BF934A15751C1A962958260, accessed Jan 31, 2011]; "Hijackings in History," article from the *Syracuse Herald Journal*, Dec 26, 1994; History Commons 9/11 timeline, "Profile: Eiffel Tower" re *Time*, Jan 2, 1995 cover story re Dec 24, 1994 GIA hijacking: "A week later, Philippine investigators breaking up the Bojinka plot in Manila find a copy of the *Time* story in bomber Ramzi Yousef's possessions." Peter Lance, *1000 Years for Revenge: International Terrorism and the FBI—the Untold Story* (New York, N.Y.: 2003), p 258 [http://www.historycommons.org/entity.jsp?entity=eiffel_tower, accessed Jun 22, 2010.]

324. U.S. Congress Joint Inquiry, *Report*, Dec 20, 2002, pp 196–97. Benjamin and Simon, *The Age of Sacred Terror*, pp 91–94, discusses Muslim apocalyptic literature of the 1990s and its fantasies of the annihilation of New York City and the destruction of the Jews, the Christians, and the United States.

325. Benjamin and Simon, *The Age of Sacred Terror*, p 4.

326. Ibid., p 6, quoting passage from Nosair's notebook.

327. Ibid., pp 7–10, 12–14.

328. Acting on a tip from an operative-turned-informant, Pakistani soldiers and U.S. agents from the Drug Enforcement Administration, the State Department Bureau of Diplomatic Security, and the FBI apprehended Ramzi Yousef at an Islamabad bed-and-breakfast owned by bin Laden on the morning of February 7, 1995. Agents raced him to an airstrip and a "specially equipped [U.S.] Air Force 707" [Benjamin and Simon, *The Age of Sacred Terror*, p 237] for transport to the United States. Wright, *The Looming Tower*, pp 204–205; Benjamin and Simon, *The Age of Sacred Terror*, pp 24–25, 237.

329. Wright, *The Looming Tower*, p 316.

330. Ibid., pp 235–36, 307–308; *The 9/11 Commission Final Report*, pp 147, 149, 153–55.

331. Wright, *The Looming Tower*, p 375; "Sources Report Death of Mohammed Atef," CNN.com, transcript of interview by CNN anchor Bill Hemmer with CNN national correspondent Mike Boettcher, Nov 16, 2001, 10:31 [a.m.?] ET [http://transcripts.cnn.com/TRANSCRIPTS/0111/16/bn.02.html, accessed Jun 17, 2011]; Khaled Dawoud, "Mohammed Atef," *The Guardian*, guardian.co.uk, Nov 19, 2001, 02.26 GMT [http://www.guardian.co.uk/news/2001/nov/19/guardianobituaries.afghanistan, accessed Jun 22, 2011, pointed out to the author by Dr. Michael Rouland, Air Force Historical Studies Office].

332. Scott Shane, "Inside a 9/11 Mastermind's Interrogation," *New York Times*, Jun 22, 2008 [http://www.nytimes.com/2008/06/22/washington/22ksm.html, accessed Jun 17, 2011]; Philip Smucker, "Al-Qa'eda chief betrayed by bin Laden's friend," *The Telegraph*, Mar 5, 2003, 12:01 a.m. GMT. [http://www.telegraph.co.uk/news/uknews/1423774/Al-Qaeda-chief-betrayed-by-bin-Ladens-friend.html, accessed Mar 25, 2011.]

333. Helene Cooper, "Obama Announces Killing of Osama bin Laden," *New York Times*, May 1, 2011, 11:29 p.m. [EDT]. [http://thelede.blogs.nytimes.com/2011/05/01/bin-laden-dead-u-s-official-says/, accessed Jun 17, 2011.]

334. Mary Beth Sheridan, "Zawahiri named new al-Qaeda leader," *Washington Post*, Jun 16, 2011. [http://www.washingtonpost.com/world/al-zawahiri-named-new-al-qaeda-leader/2011/06/16/A GNk87WH_story.html, accessed Jun 17, 2011.]

335. AQAP was created in January 2009.

336. Al Baker and William K. Rashbaum, "Police Find Car Bomb in Times Square," *New York Times*, NYTimes.com, May 1, 2010. [http://www.nytimes.com/2010/05/02/nyregion/02timessquare.html?pagewanted=print, accessed Mar 7, 2011]; David Montero, "US-born cleric inspired Times Square

bomber Faisal Shahzad," *Christian Science Monitor*, CSMonitor.com, posted May 7, 2010 at 8:41 a.m. EDT. [http://www.csmonitor.com/layout/set/print/content/view/print/299705, accessed Mar 7, 2011]; Chad Bray, "Times Square Plotter Gets Life Term," *Wall Street Journal*, WSJ.com, Oct 5, 2010 [http://online.wsj.com/article/SB10001424052748704469004575533902050370826.html?mod=dje-malertNYnews#printMode, accessed Mar 7, 2011.]

337. Philip Sherwell and Alex Spillius, "Fort Hood shooting: Texas army killer linked to September 11 terrorists," *The Telegraph*, Nov 7, 2009, 8:17 p.m. GMT [Greenwich Mean Time]. [http://www.telegraph.co.uk/news/worldnews/northamerica/usa/6521758/Fort-Hood-shooting-Texas-army-killer-linked-to-September-11-terrorists.html, accessed Mar 4, 2011.]

338. Tabular information on all four flights' transponders from *The 9/11 Commission Final Report*, p 454, endnote 54, citing FAA report, "Summary of Air Traffic Hijack Events: September 11, 2001."

339. Perhaps a typographical error. Shown as 1224:56 [UTC] [0824:56 a.m. EDT] in Joseph A. Gregor, "Specialist's Report," Air Traffic Control Recording: American Airlines Flight 11, Dec 21, 2001. National Transportation Safety Board, Vehicle Recorders Division, Washington, D.C. The National Security Archive, The September 11th Sourcebooks, National Security Archive Electronic Briefing Book (hereinafter NSAEBB) No. 196, posted Aug 11, 2006, Document 5. [http://www.gwu.edu/~nsarchiv/NSAEBB/NSAEBB196/doc05.pdf, accessed Apr 30, 2008.]

340. Precise time not mentioned in *The 9/11 Commission Final Report*. Source here is Department of Transportation, Federal Aviation Administration, "Summary of Air Traffic Hijack Events, September 11, 2001," Sep 17, 2001, 6:30 a.m. The National Security Archive, The September 11th Sourcebooks, NSAEBB No. 165, posted Sep 9, 2005, Document 7. [http://www.gwu.edu/~ nsarchiv/NSAEBB/NSAEBB165/faa7.pdf, accessed Apr 24, 2009.] Time shown as 08:26:30 a.m. EDT in Jim Ritter, Chief, Vehicle Performance Division, "Flight Path Study—American Airlines Flight 11," Feb 19, 2002. National Transportation Safety Board, Office of Research and Engineering, Washington, D.C. The National Security Archive, The September 11th Sourcebooks, NSAEBB No. 196, posted Aug 11, 2006, Document 1. [http://www.gwu.edu/~nsarchiv/NSAEBB/NSAEBB196/doc01.pdf, accessed Apr 30, 2008.]

341. Time shown as 1233:59 [UTC] [0833:59 a.m. EDT] in Gregor, "Specialist's Report," ATC Recording: American Airlines Flight 11, NTSB, NSAEBB No. 196, Doc 5.